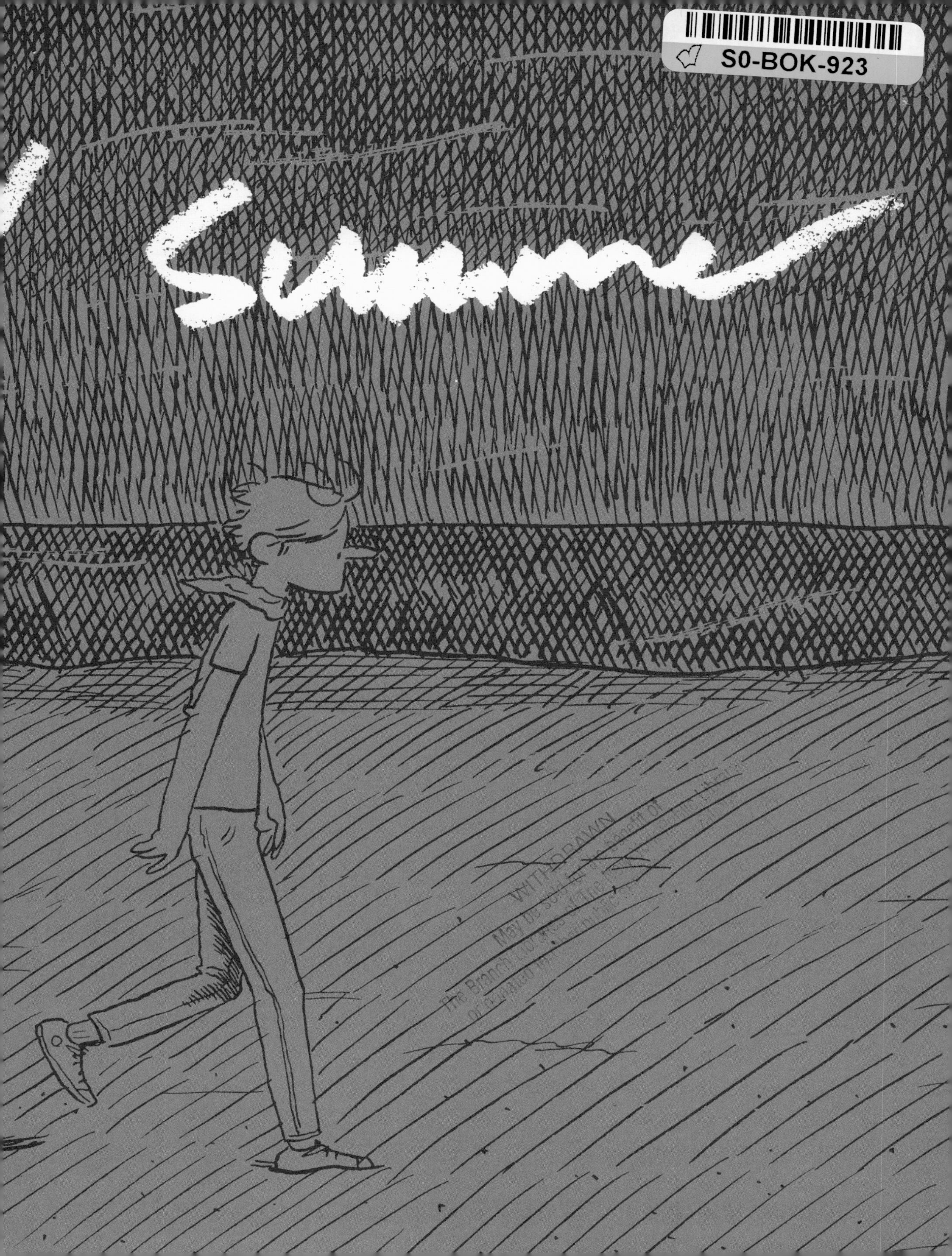

Celebrated Summer

CHARLES FORSMAN

FANTAGRAPHICS BOOKS
SEATTLE, WA, USA

FOR BUDDY AND J.C.

ISBN 978-1-60699-685-0
FIRST PRINTING: SEPTEMBER, 2013

PRINTED IN CHINA

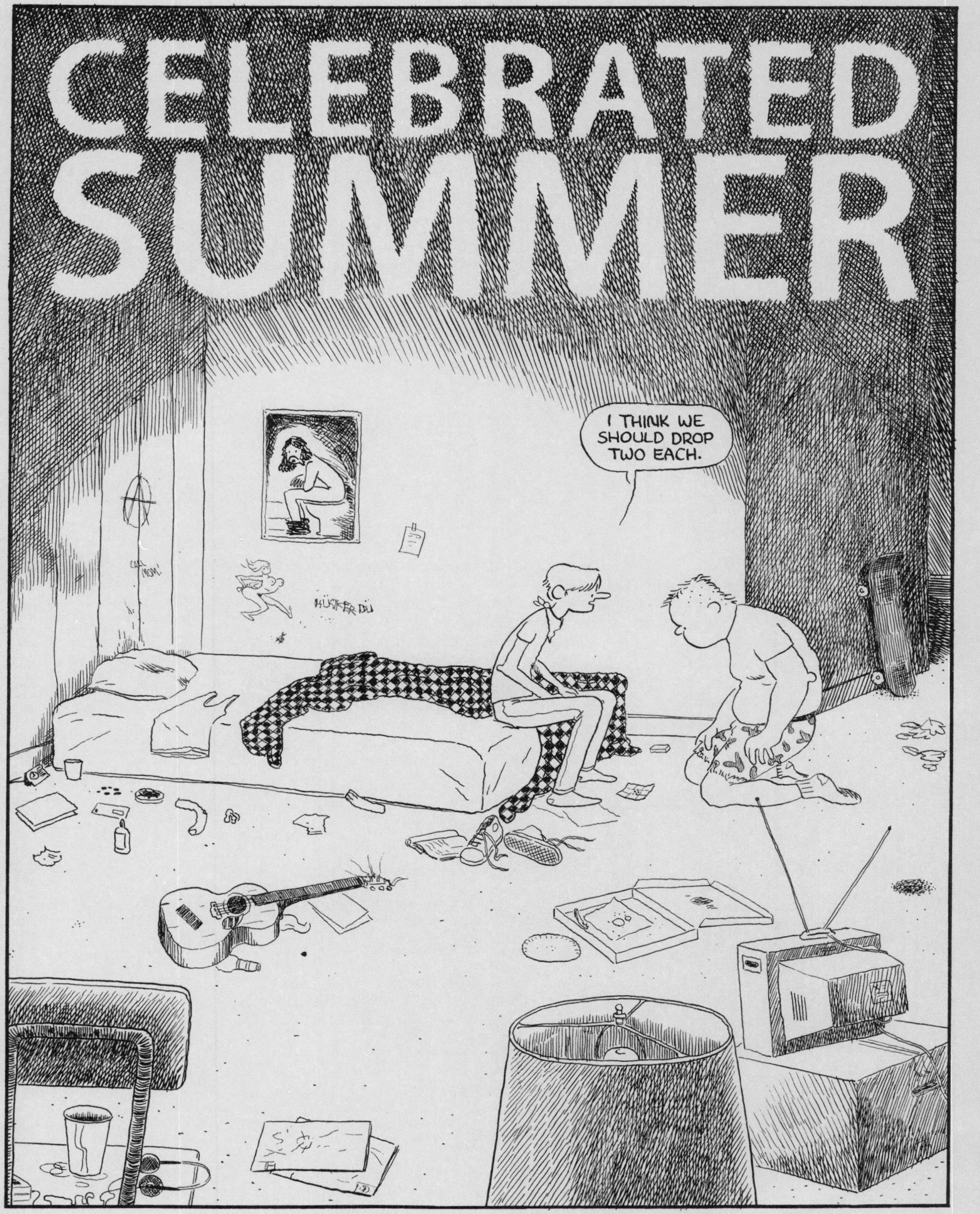
CELEBRATED SUMMER
I THINK WE SHOULD DROP TWO EACH.
HÜSKER DÜ

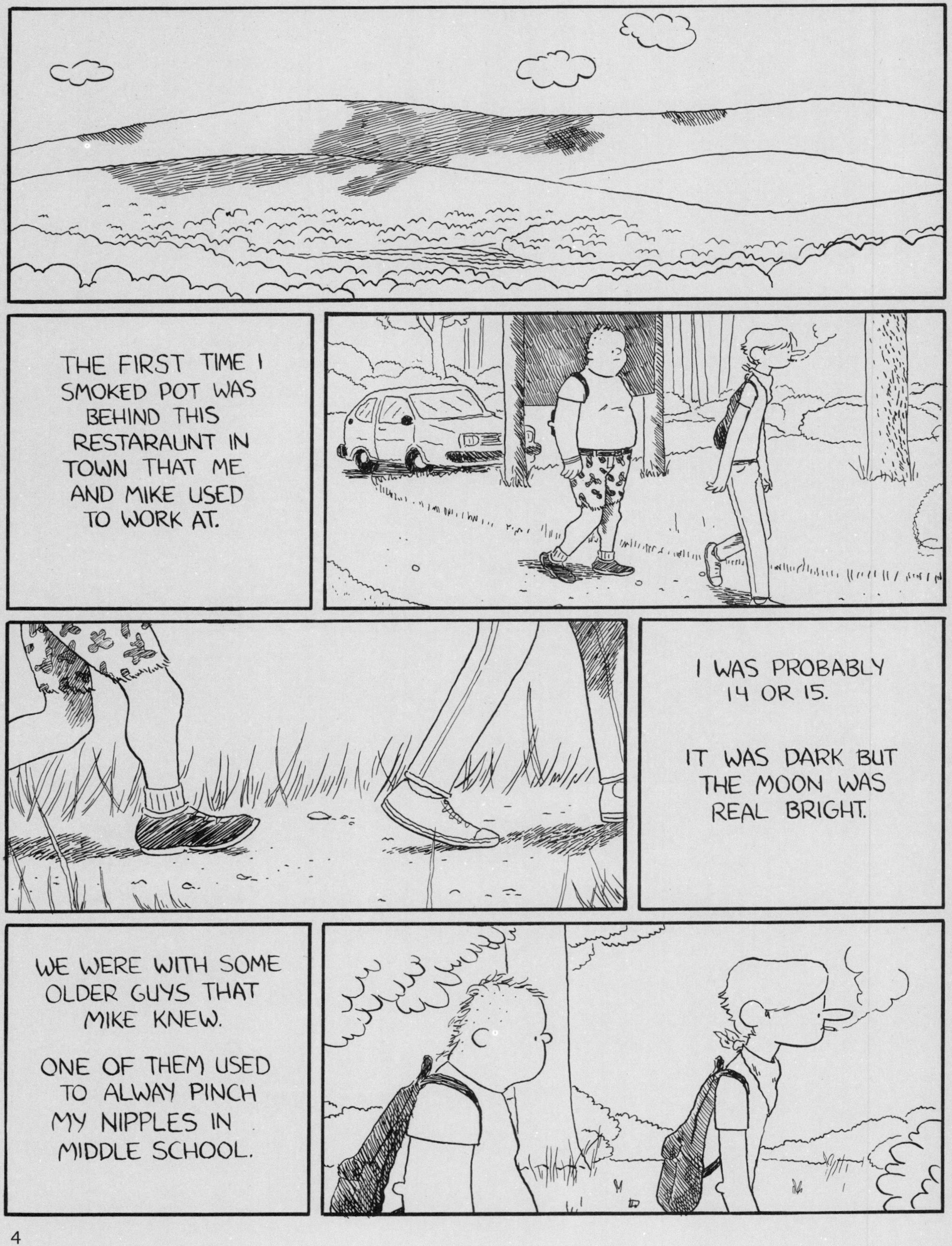
THE FIRST TIME I SMOKED POT WAS BEHIND THIS RESTARAUNT IN TOWN THAT ME AND MIKE USED TO WORK AT.
I WAS PROBABLY 14 OR 15.
IT WAS DARK BUT THE MOON WAS REAL BRIGHT.
WE WERE WITH SOME OLDER GUYS THAT MIKE KNEW.
ONE OF THEM USED TO ALWAY PINCH MY NIPPLES IN MIDDLE SCHOOL.

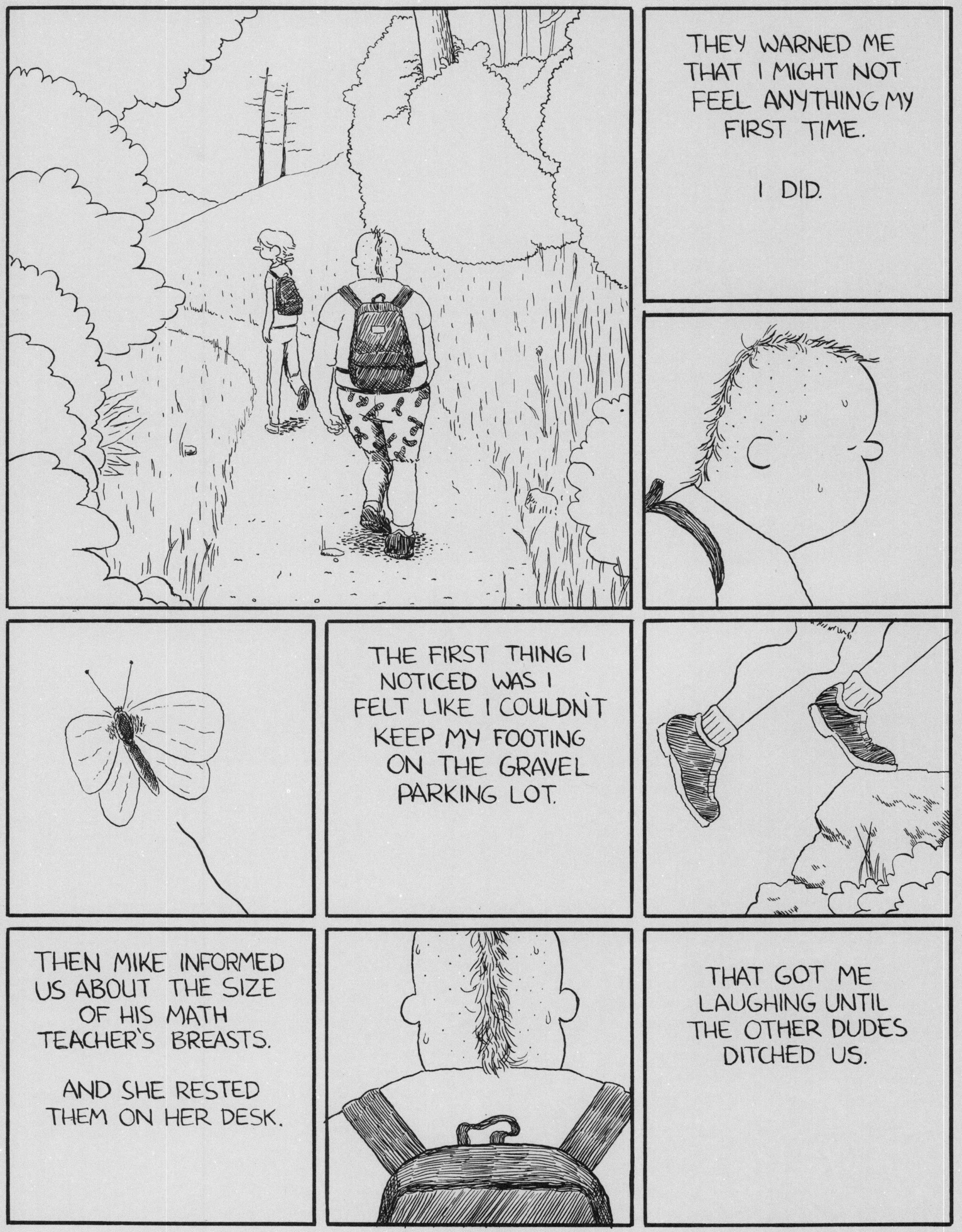
THEY WARNED ME THAT I MIGHT NOT FEEL ANYTHING MY FIRST TIME.
I DID.
THE FIRST THING I NOTICED WAS I FELT LIKE I COULDN'T KEEP MY FOOTING ON THE GRAVEL PARKING LOT.
THEN MIKE INFORMED US ABOUT THE SIZE OF HIS MATH TEACHER'S BREASTS.
AND SHE RESTED THEM ON HER DESK.
THAT GOT ME LAUGHING UNTIL THE OTHER DUDES DITCHED US.

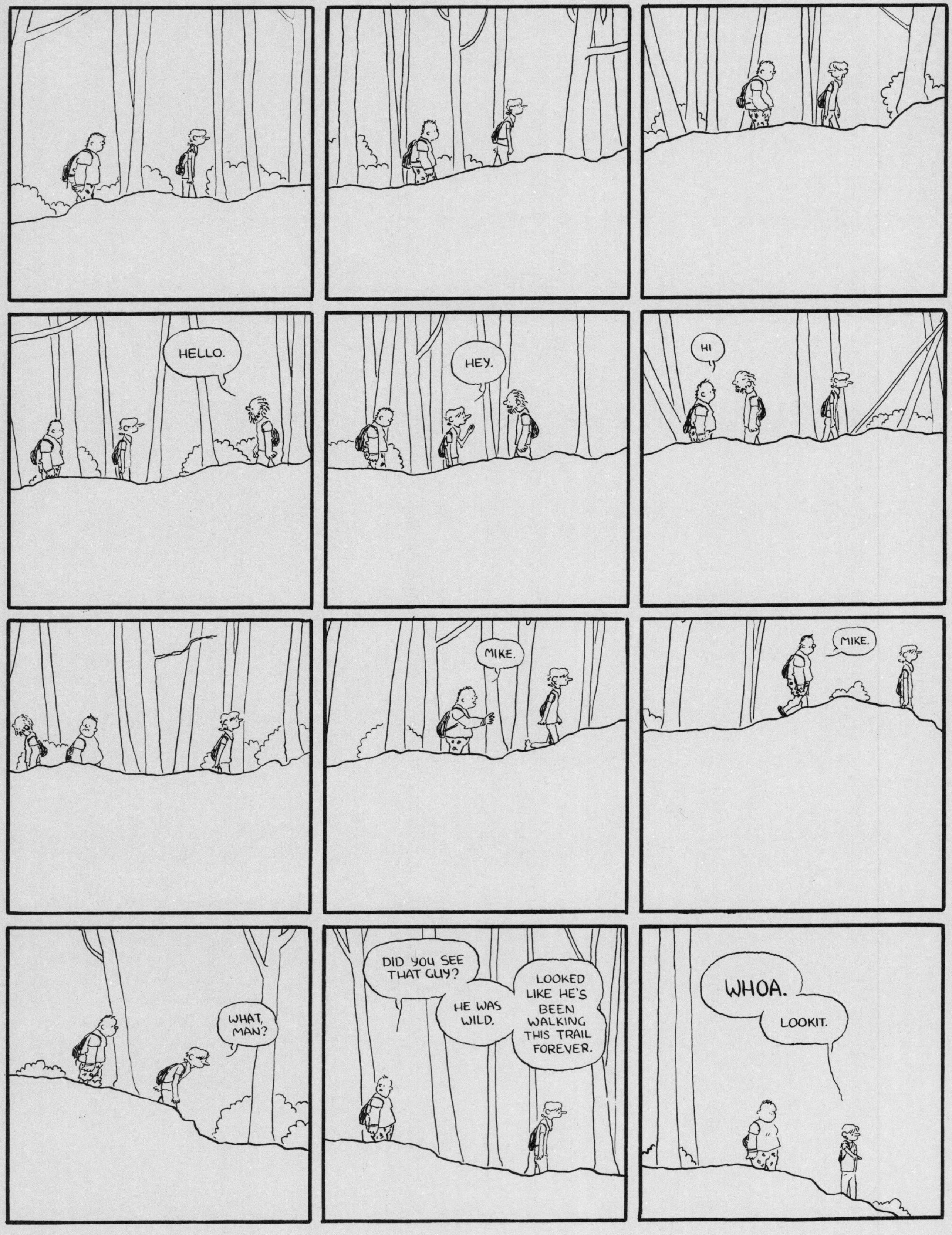
HELLO.
HEY.
HI
MIKE.
MIKE.
WHAT, MAN?
DID YOU SEE THAT GUY?
HE WAS WILD.
LOOKED LIKE HE'S BEEN WALKING THIS TRAIL FOREVER.
WHOA.
LOOKIT.

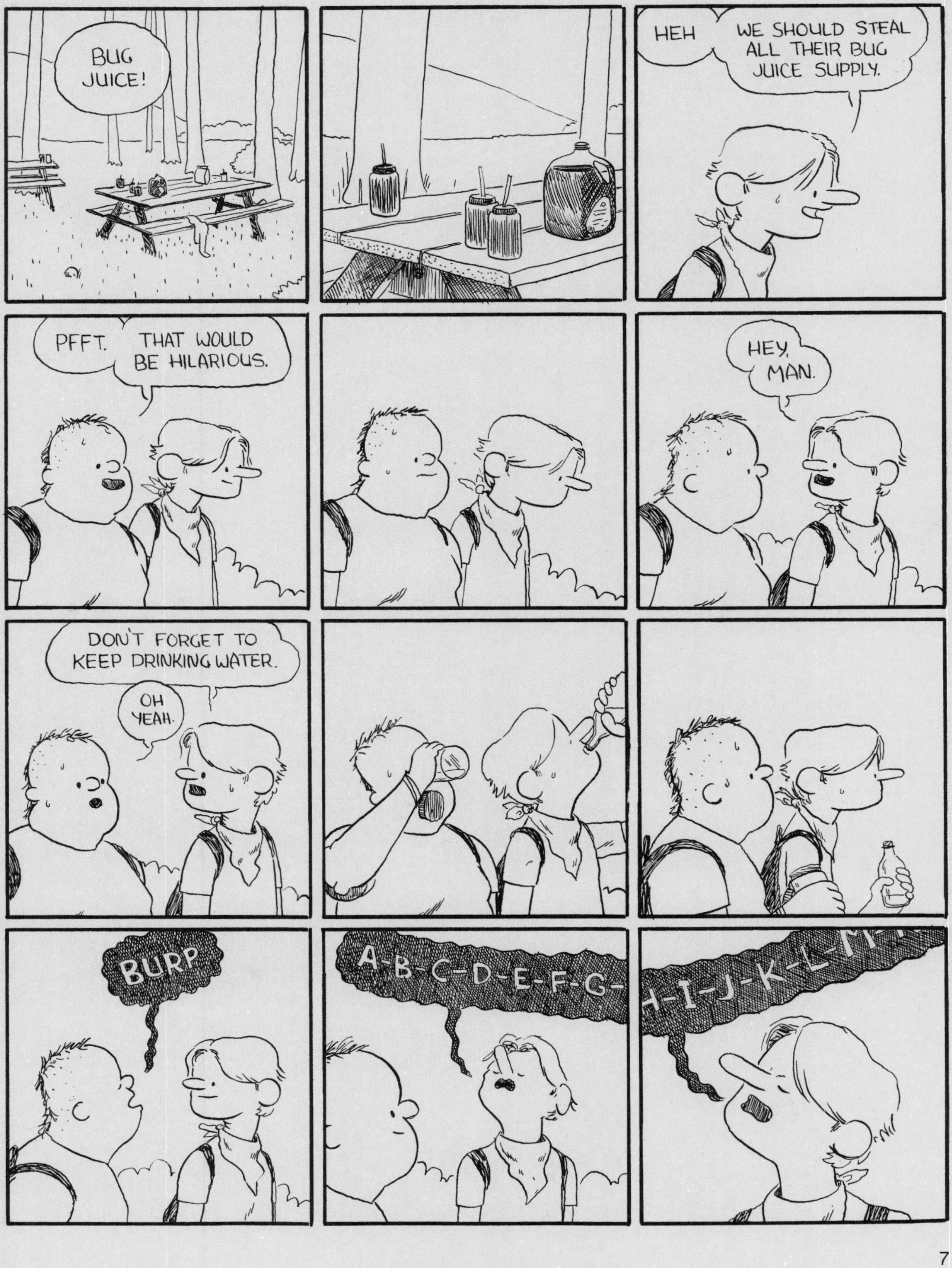
BUG JUICE!
HEH
WE SHOULD STEAL ALL THEIR BUG JUICE SUPPLY.
PFFT.
THAT WOULD BE HILARIOUS.
HEY, MAN.
DON'T FORGET TO KEEP DRINKING WATER.
OH YEAH.
BURP
A-B-C-D-E-F-G-
H-I-J-K-L-M-

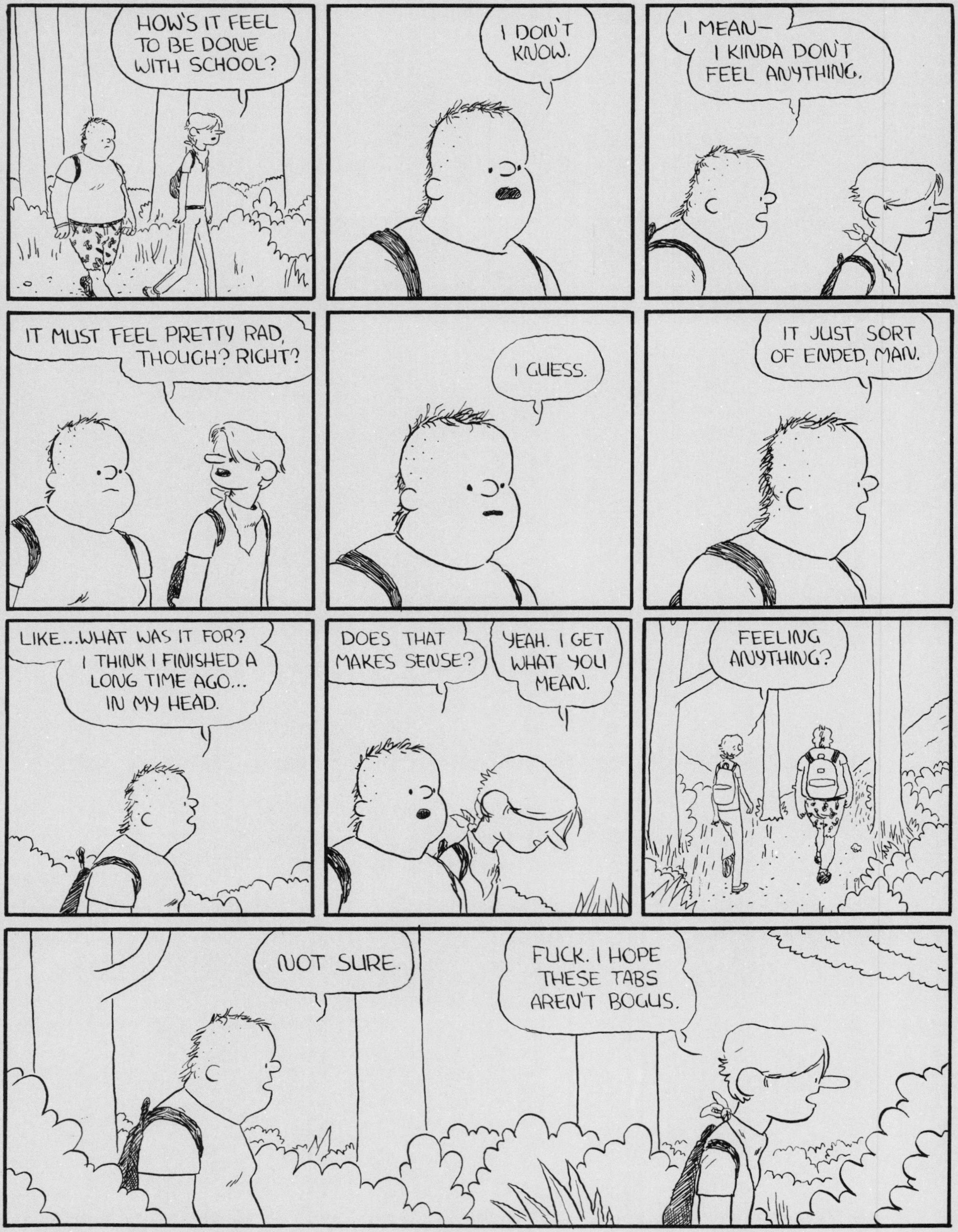
HOW'S IT FEEL TO BE DONE WITH SCHOOL?
I DON'T KNOW.
I MEAN— I KINDA DON'T FEEL ANYTHING.
IT MUST FEEL PRETTY RAD, THOUGH? RIGHT?
I GUESS.
IT JUST SORT OF ENDED, MAN.
LIKE...WHAT WAS IT FOR? I THINK I FINISHED A LONG TIME AGO... IN MY HEAD.
DOES THAT MAKES SENSE?
YEAH. I GET WHAT YOU MEAN.
FEELING ANYTHING?
NOT SURE.
FUCK. I HOPE THESE TABS AREN'T BOGUS.

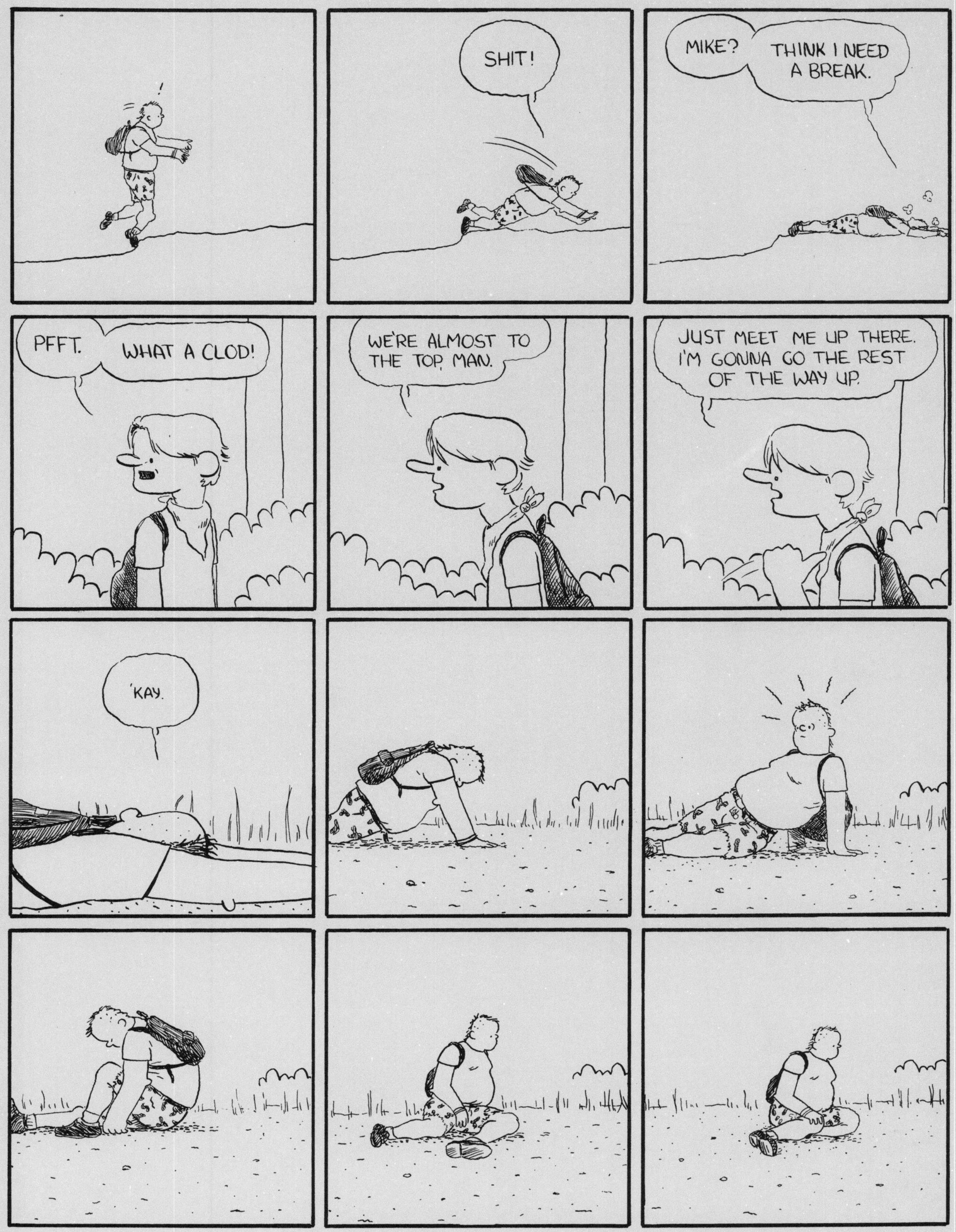
!
SHIT!
MIKE?
THINK I NEED A BREAK.
PFFT.
WHAT A CLOD!
WE'RE ALMOST TO THE TOP, MAN.
JUST MEET ME UP THERE. I'M GONNA GO THE REST OF THE WAY UP.
'KAY.

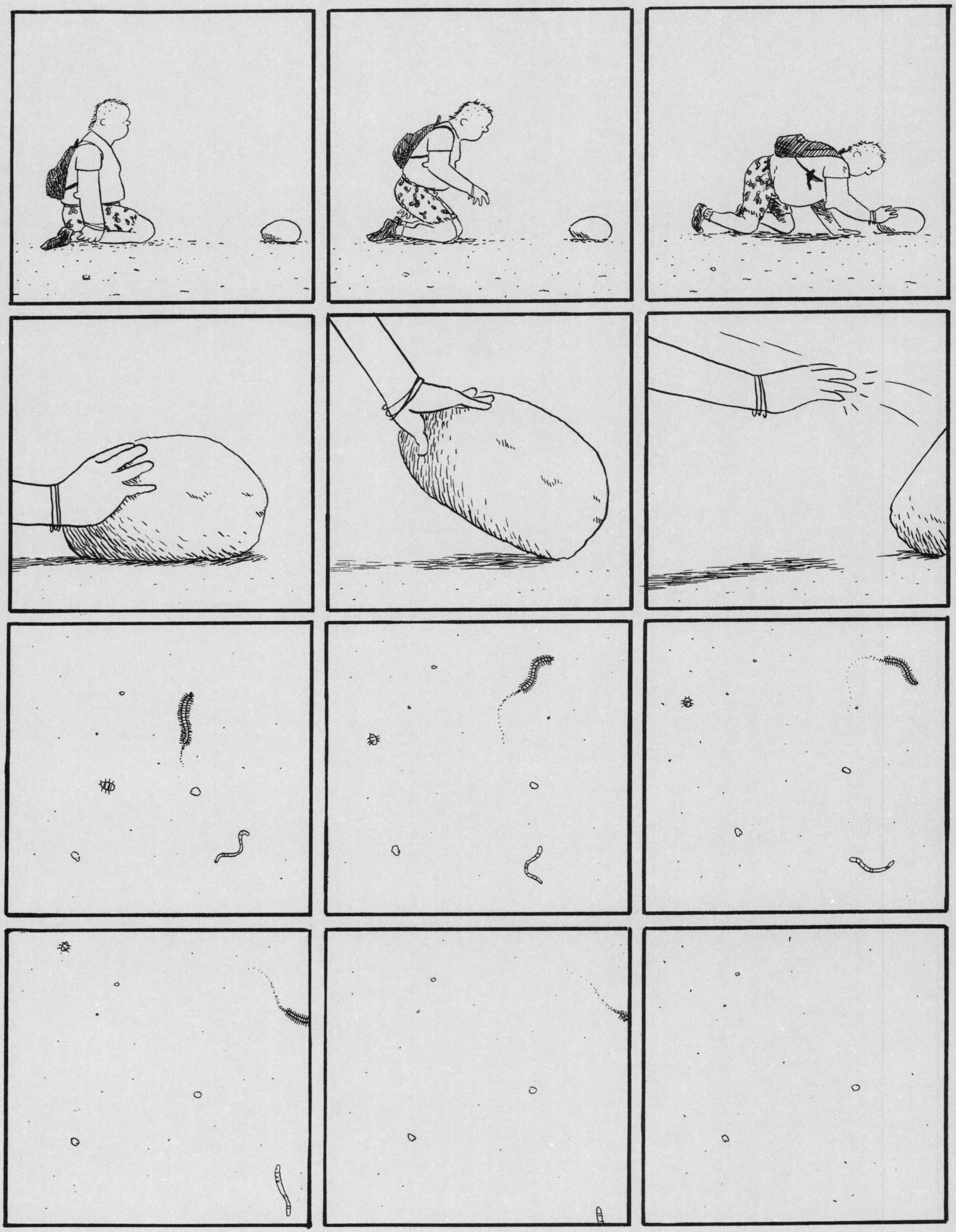

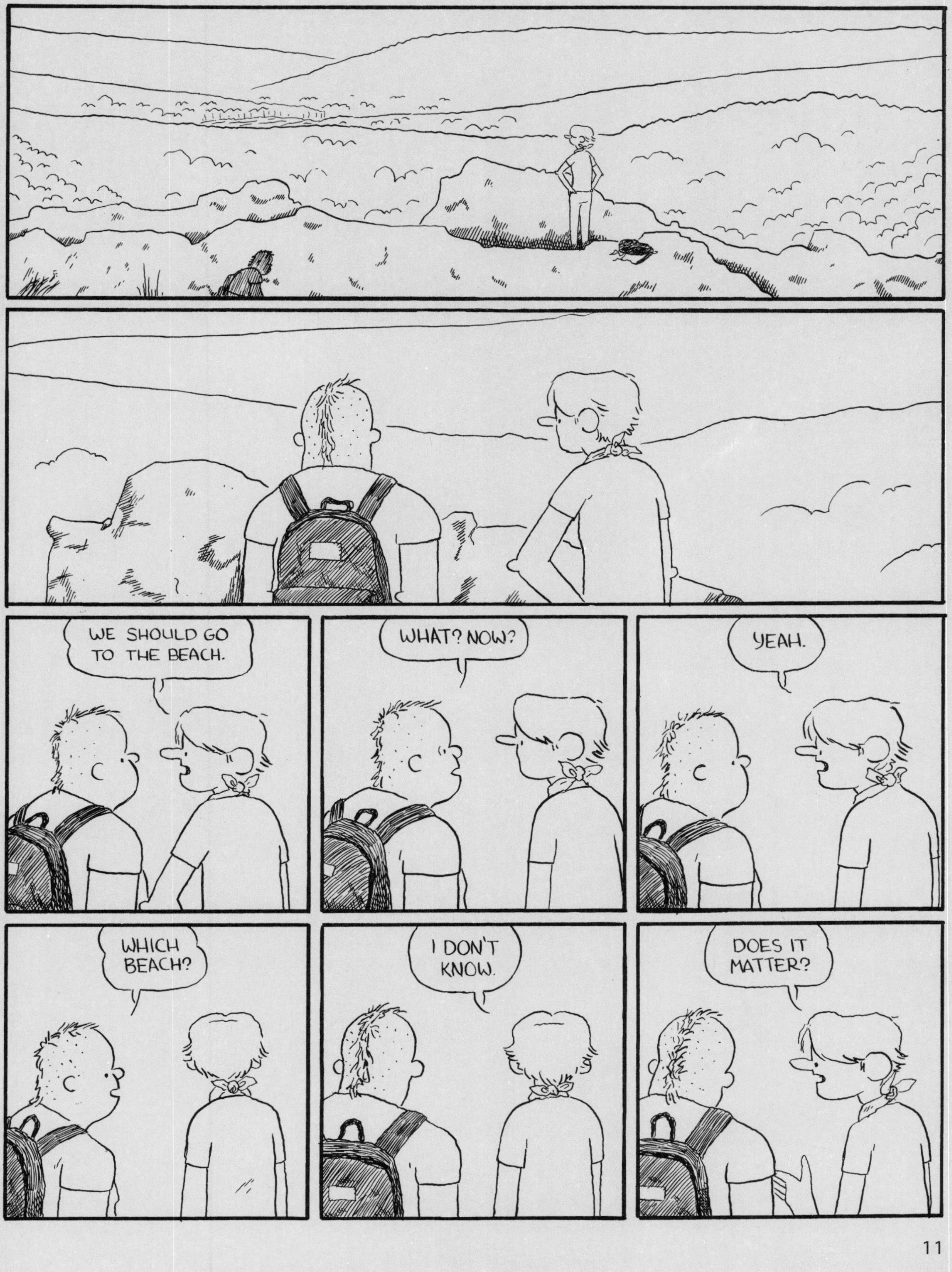
WE SHOULD GO TO THE BEACH.
WHAT? NOW?
YEAH.
WHICH BEACH?
I DON'T KNOW.
DOES IT MATTER?

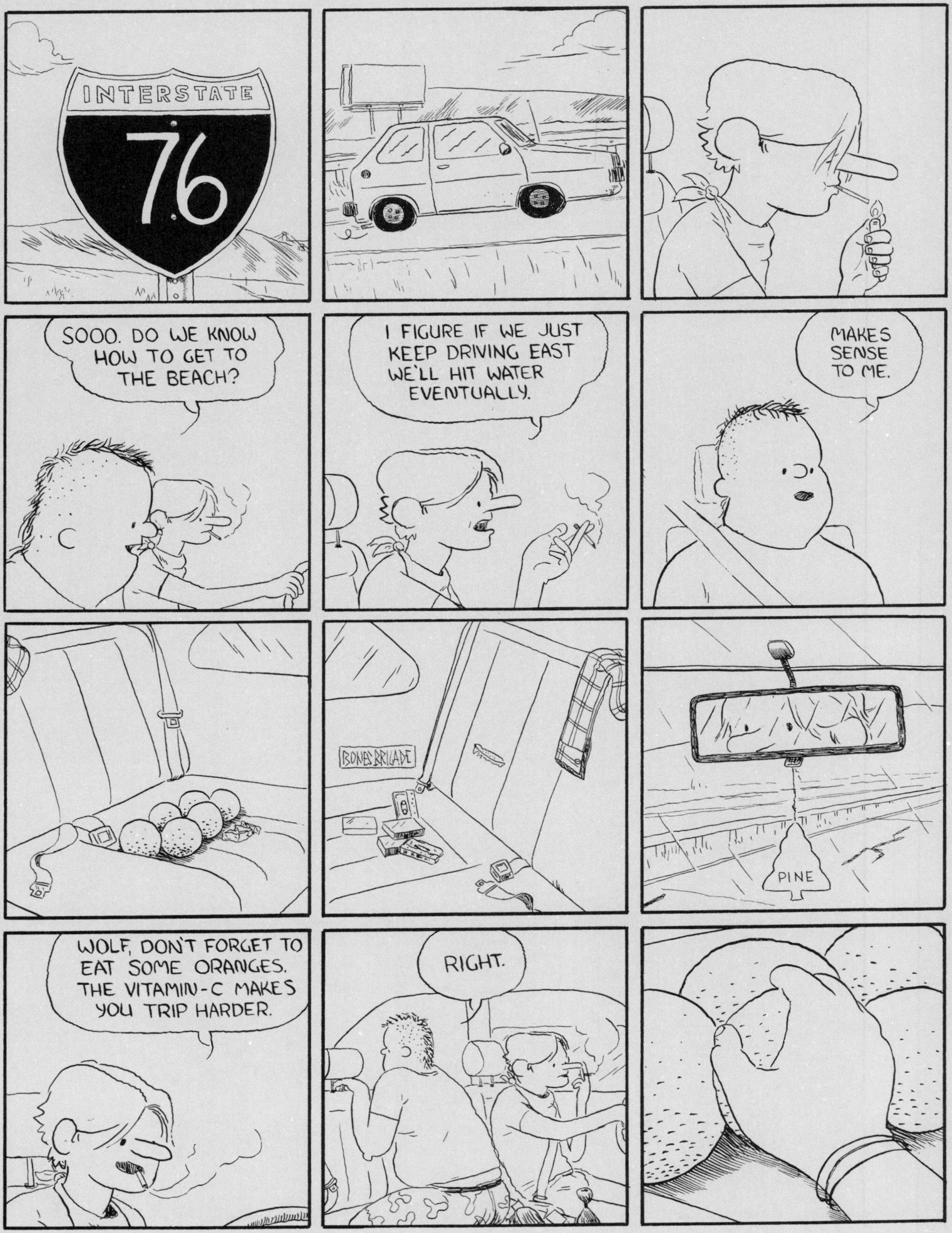
INTERSTATE
76
SOOO. DO WE KNOW HOW TO GET TO THE BEACH?
I FIGURE IF WE JUST KEEP DRIVING EAST WE'LL HIT WATER EVENTUALLY.
MAKES SENSE TO ME.
BONES BRIGADE
PINE
WOLF, DON'T FORGET TO EAT SOME ORANGES. THE VITAMIN-C MAKES YOU TRIP HARDER.
RIGHT.

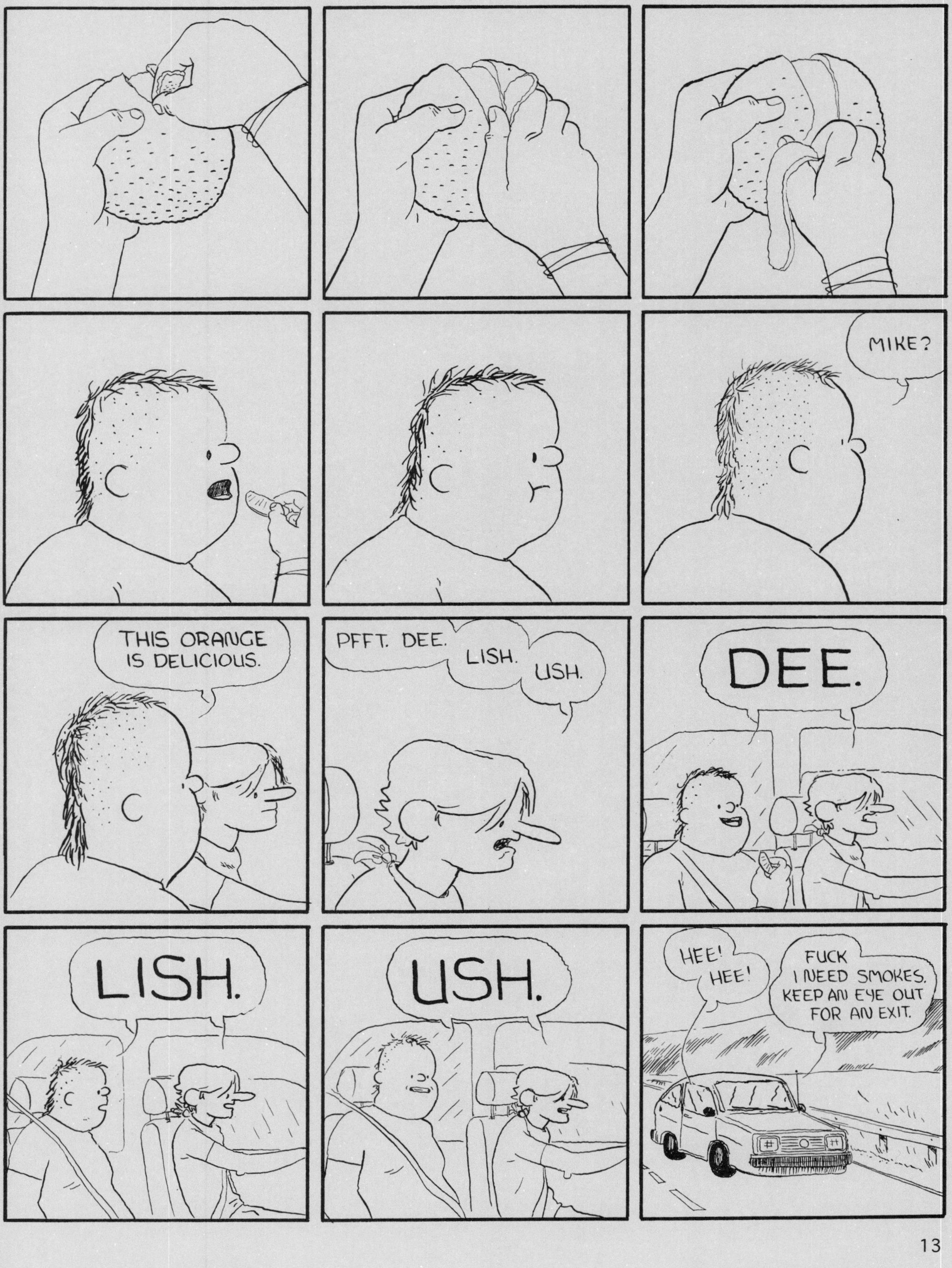
MIKE?
THIS ORANGE IS DELICIOUS.
PFFT. DEE.
LISH.
USH.
DEE.
LISH.
USH.
HEE! HEE!
FUCK I NEED SMOKES. KEEP AN EYE OUT FOR AN EXIT.

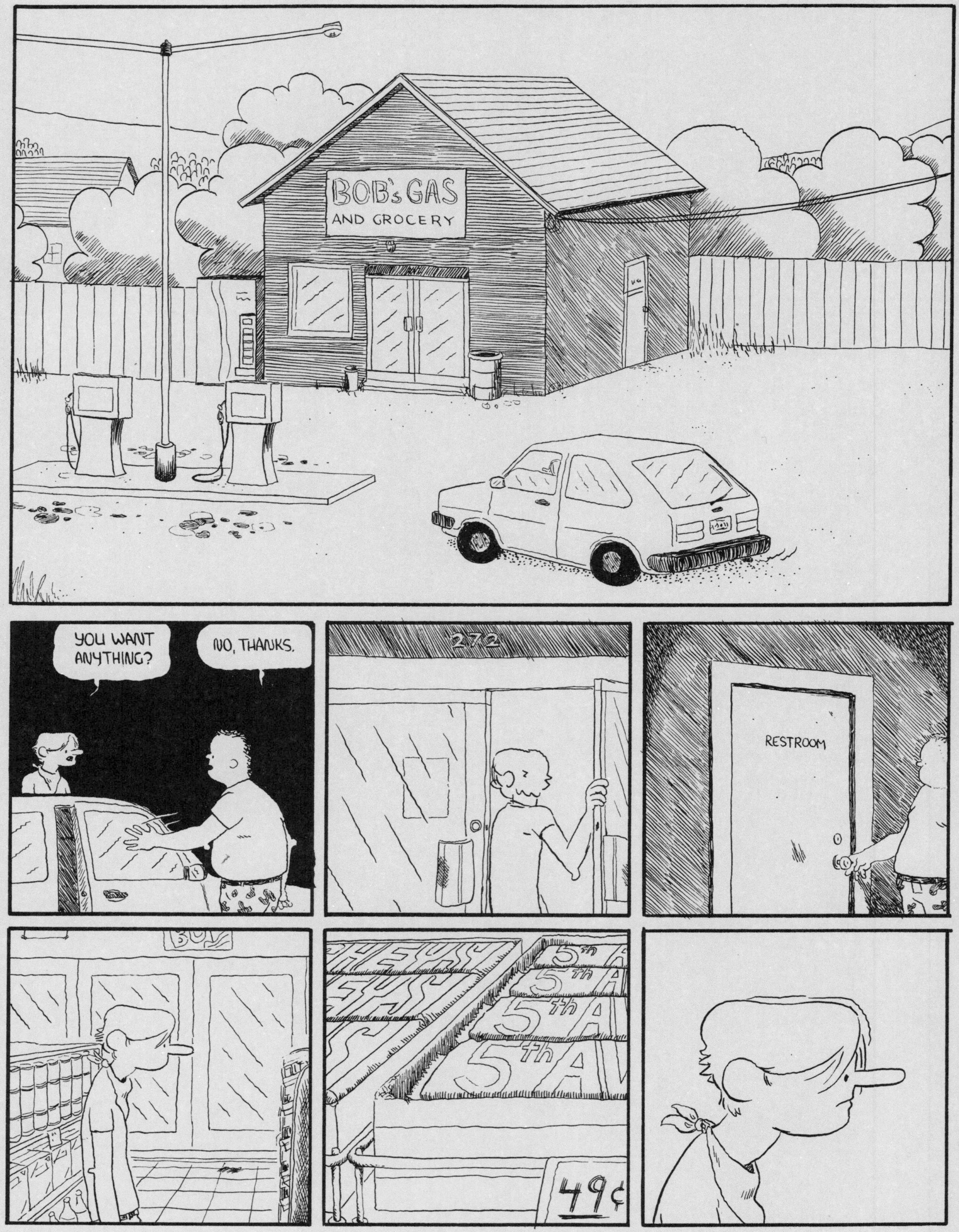
BOB's GAS
AND GROCERY
YOU WANT ANYTHING?
NO, THANKS.
272
RESTROOM
5th A
49¢

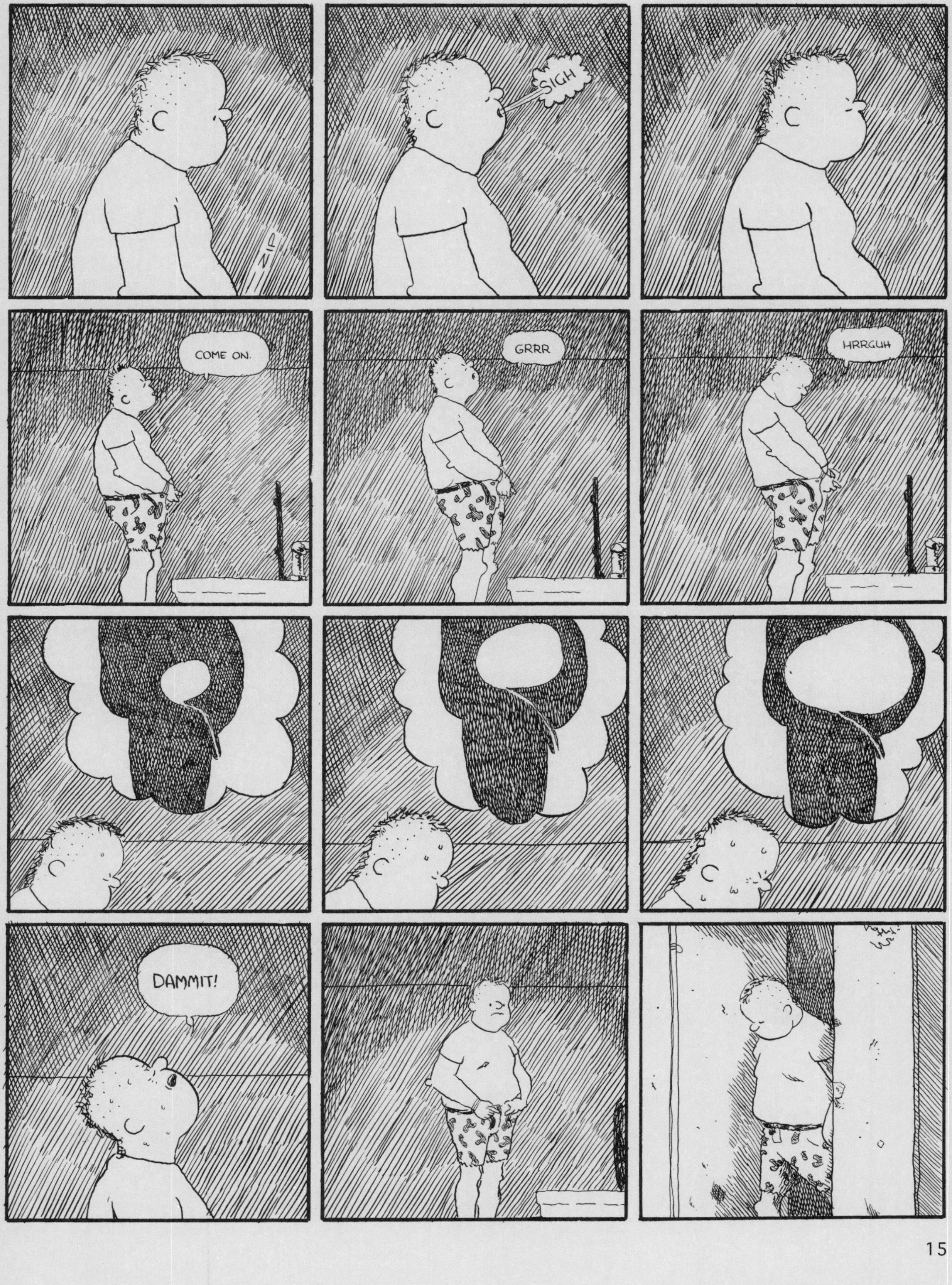
ZIP
SIGH
COME ON.
GRRR
HRRGUH
DAMMIT!

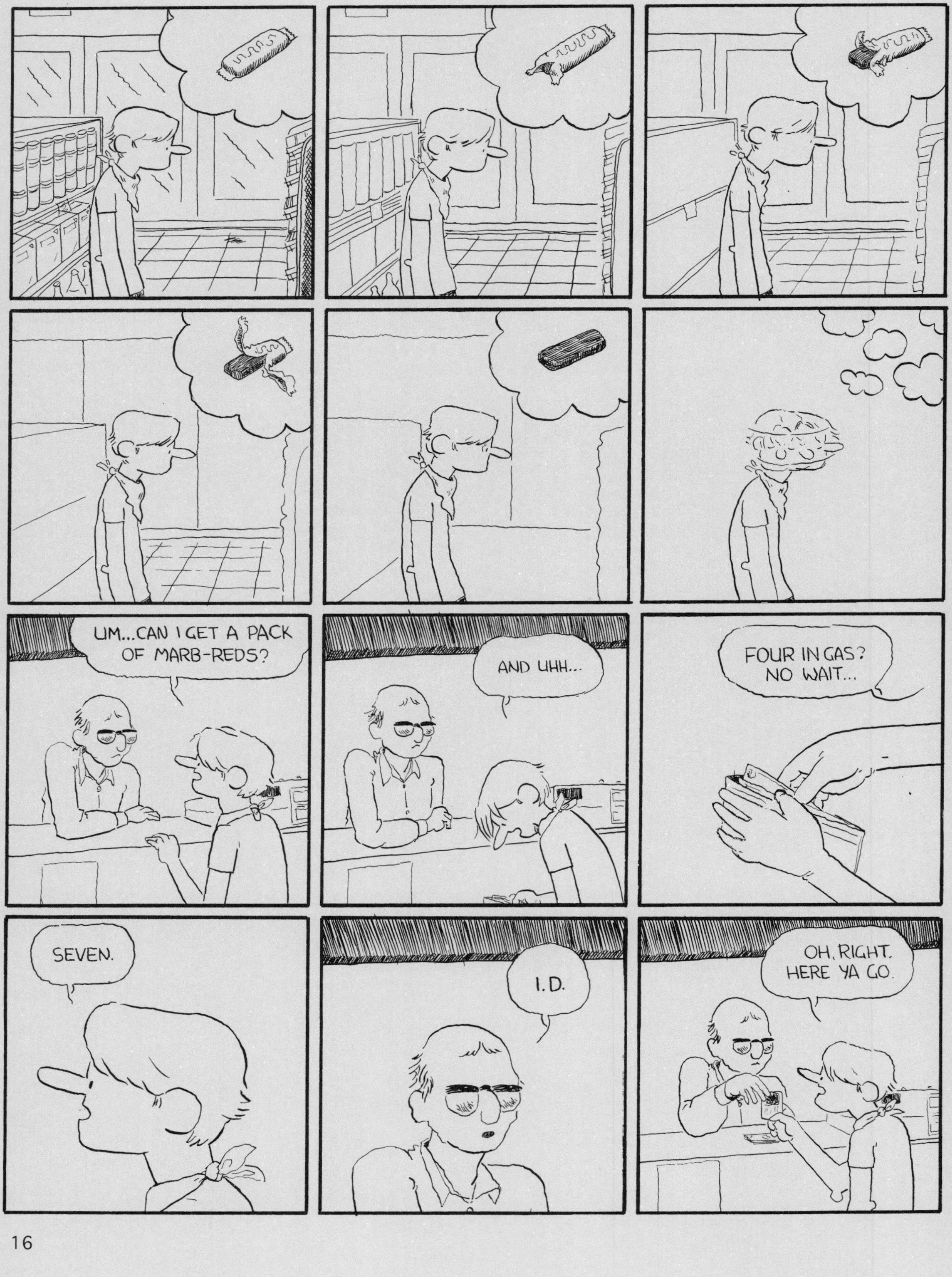
UM...CAN I GET A PACK OF MARB-REDS?
AND UHH...
FOUR IN GAS? NO WAIT...
SEVEN.
I.D.
OH, RIGHT. HERE YA GO.

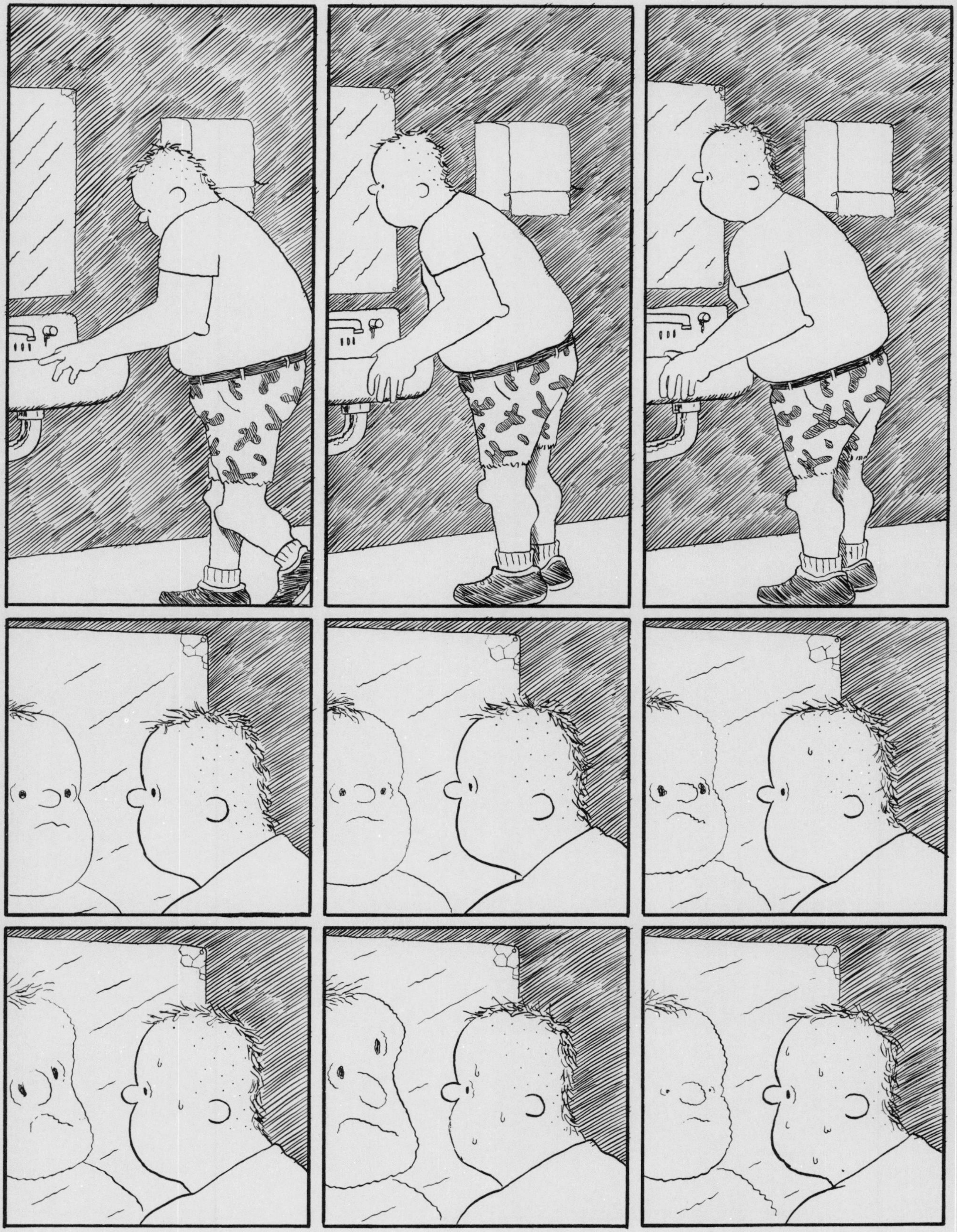

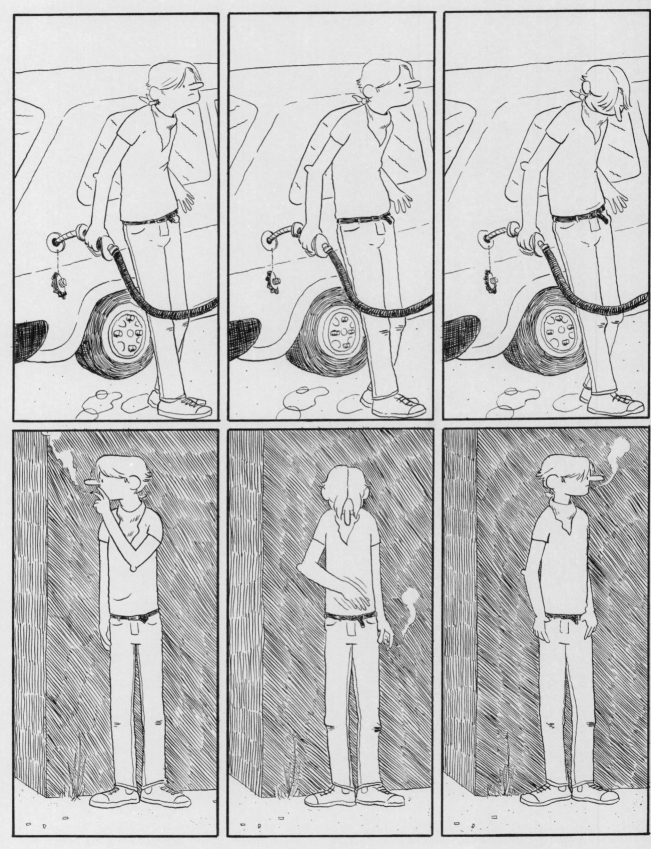

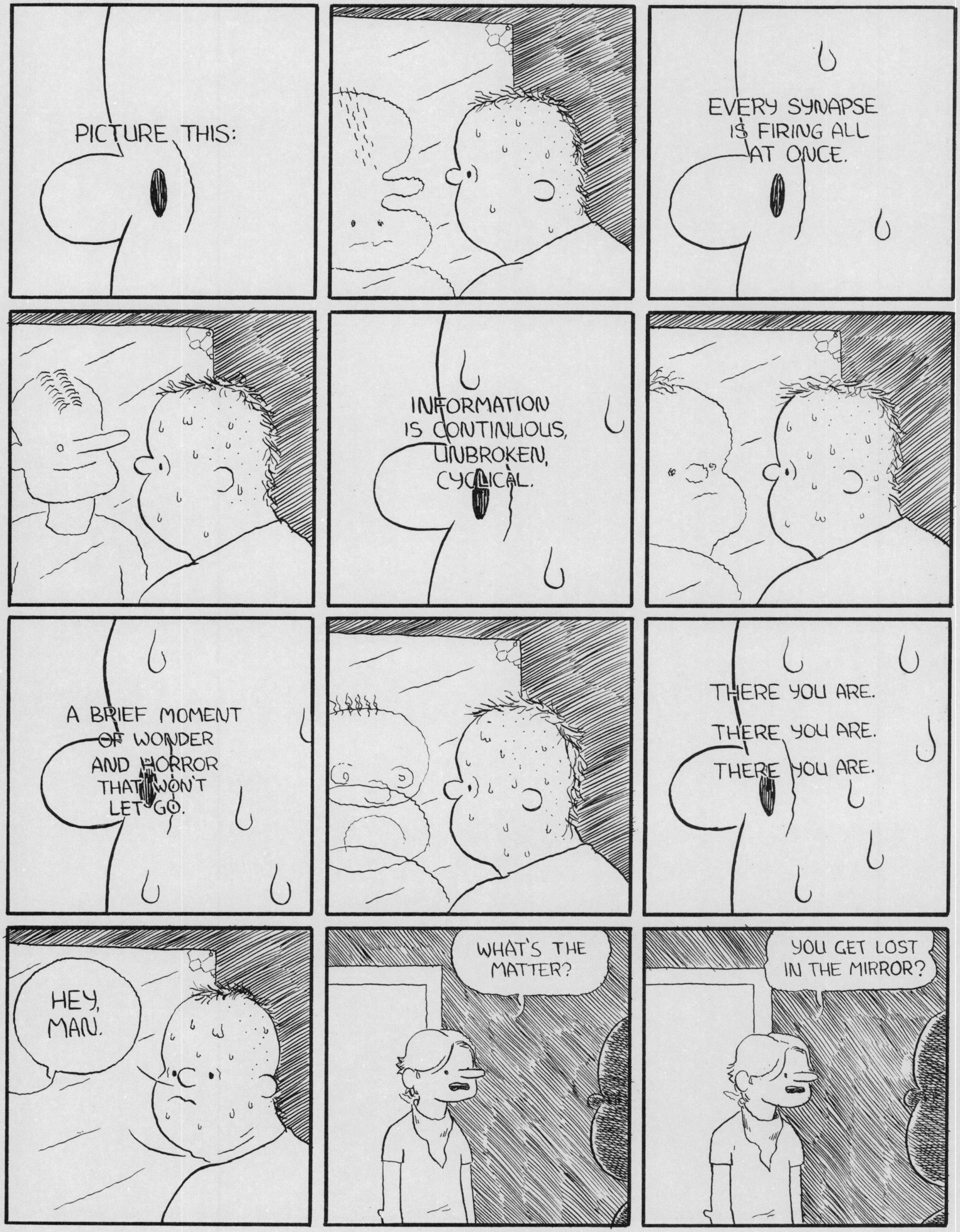
PICTURE THIS:
EVERY SYNAPSE IS FIRING ALL AT ONCE.
INFORMATION IS CONTINUOUS, UNBROKEN, CYCLICAL.
A BRIEF MOMENT OF WONDER AND HORROR THAT WON'T LET GO.
THERE YOU ARE.
THERE YOU ARE.
THERE YOU ARE.
HEY, MAN.
WHAT'S THE MATTER?
YOU GET LOST IN THE MIRROR?

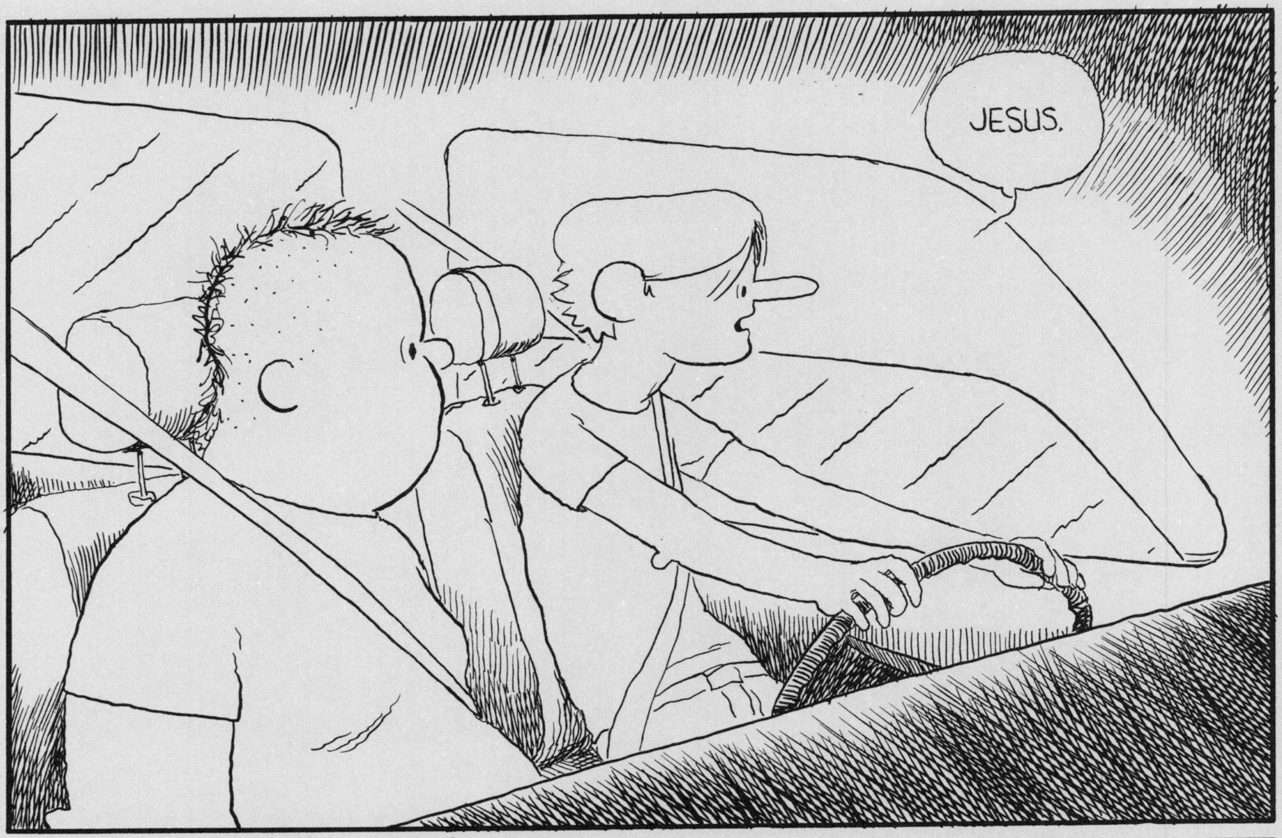
JESUS.

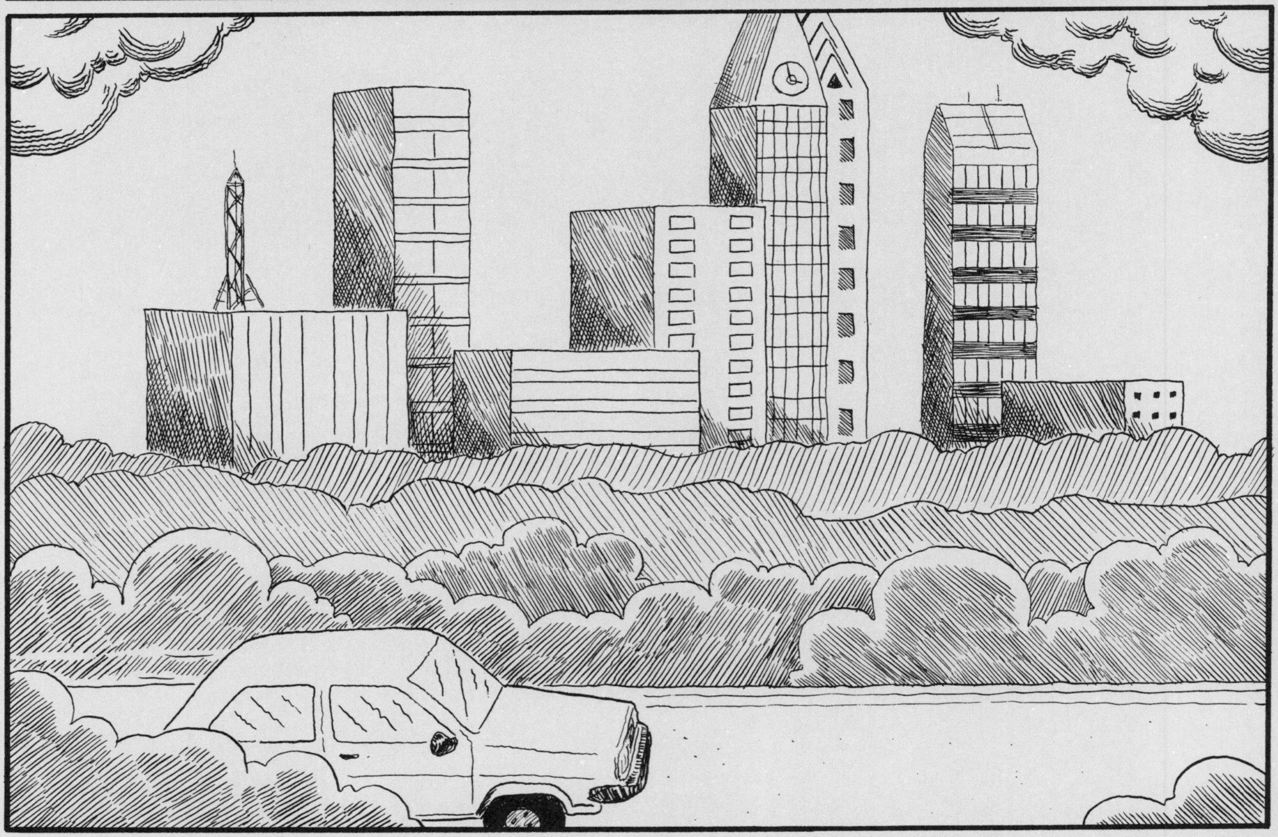

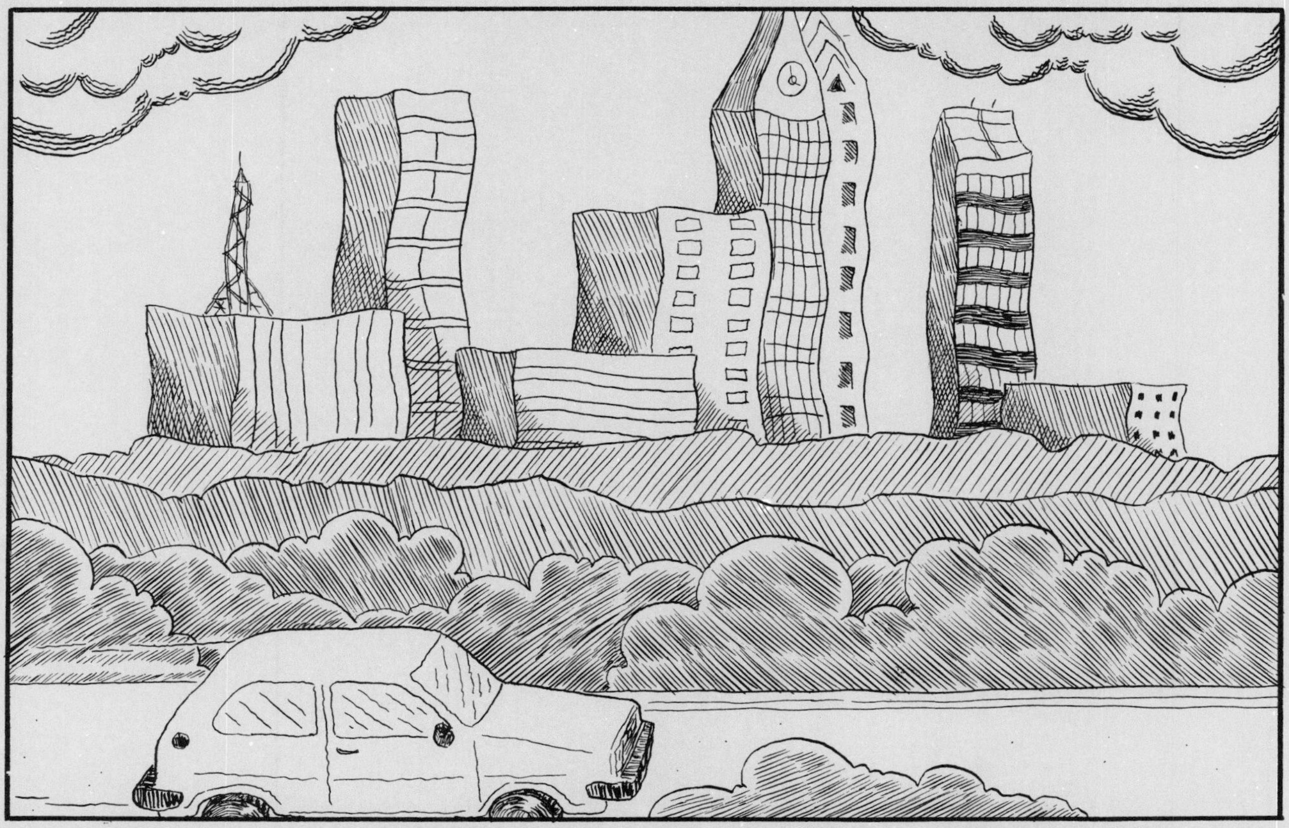

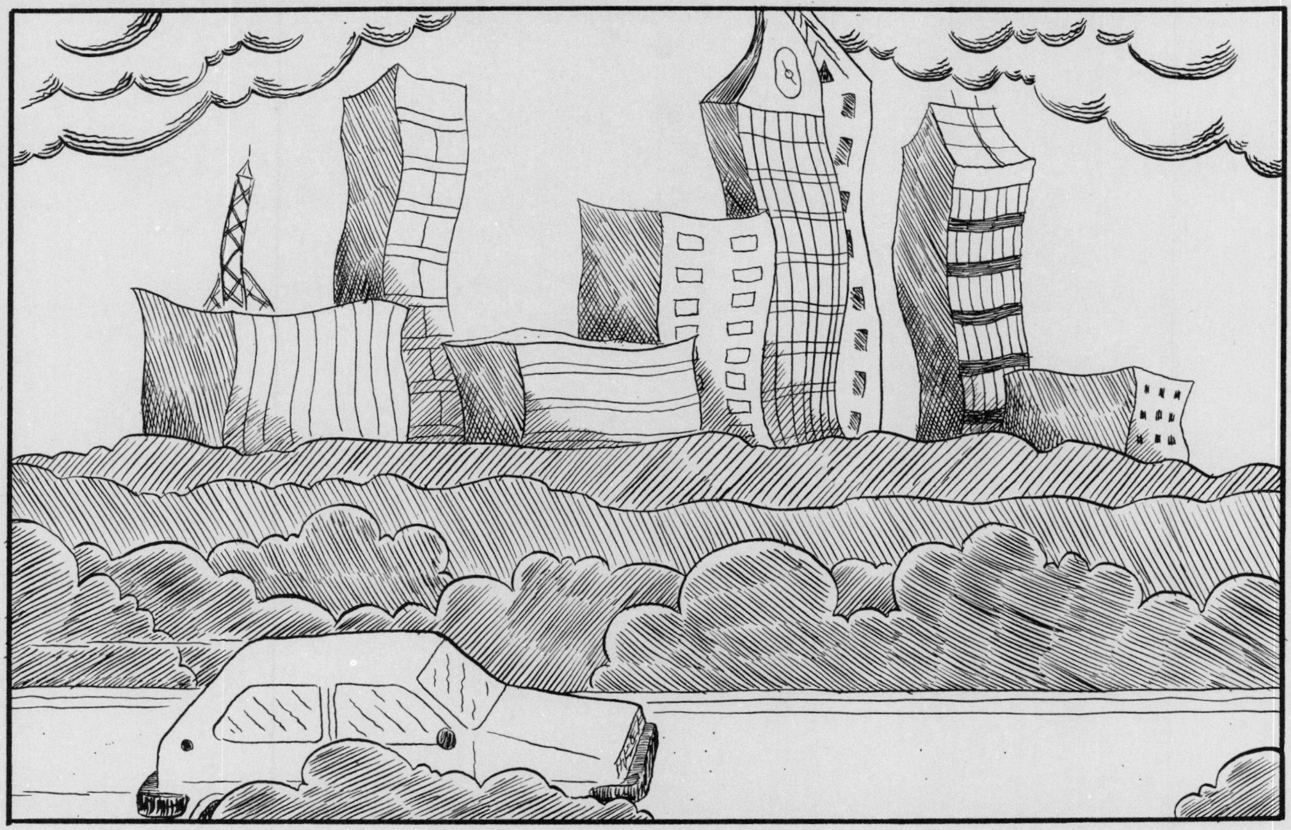

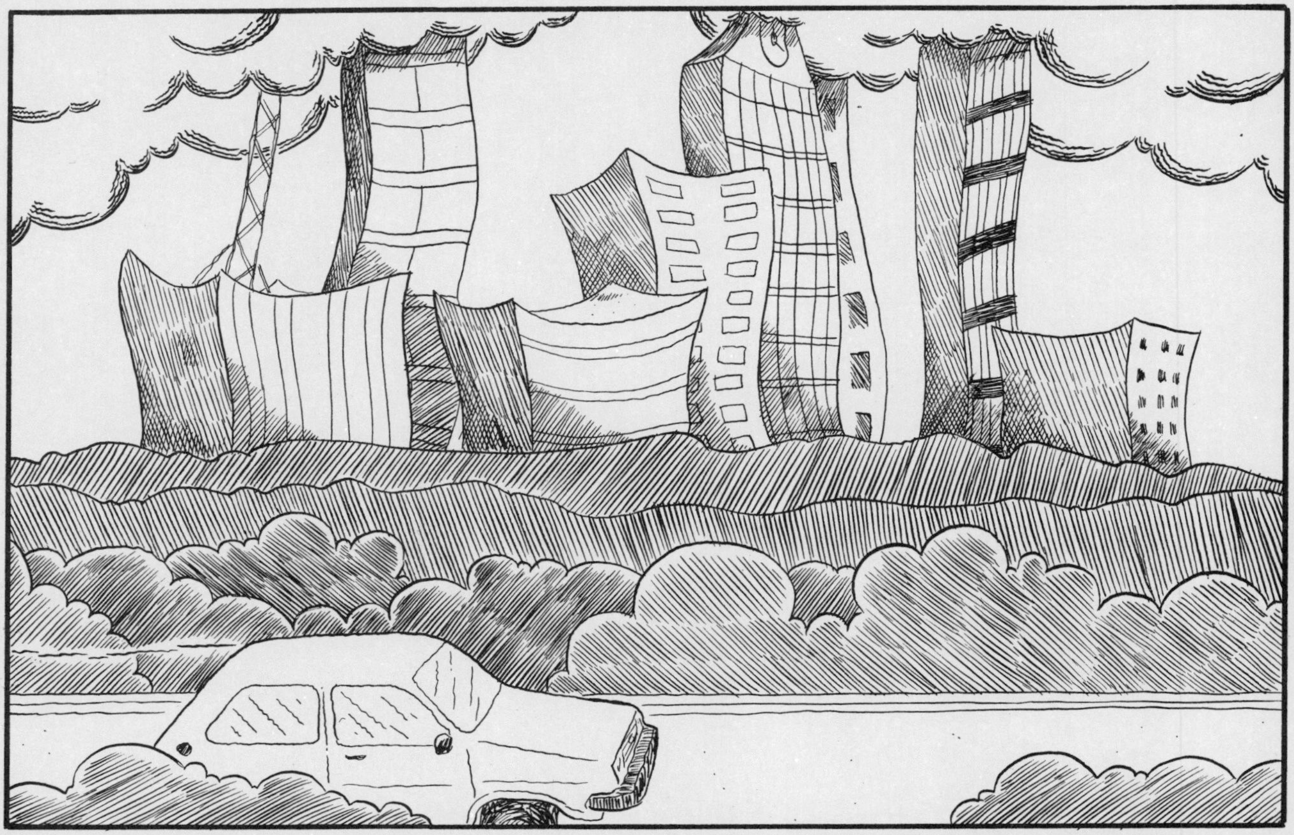

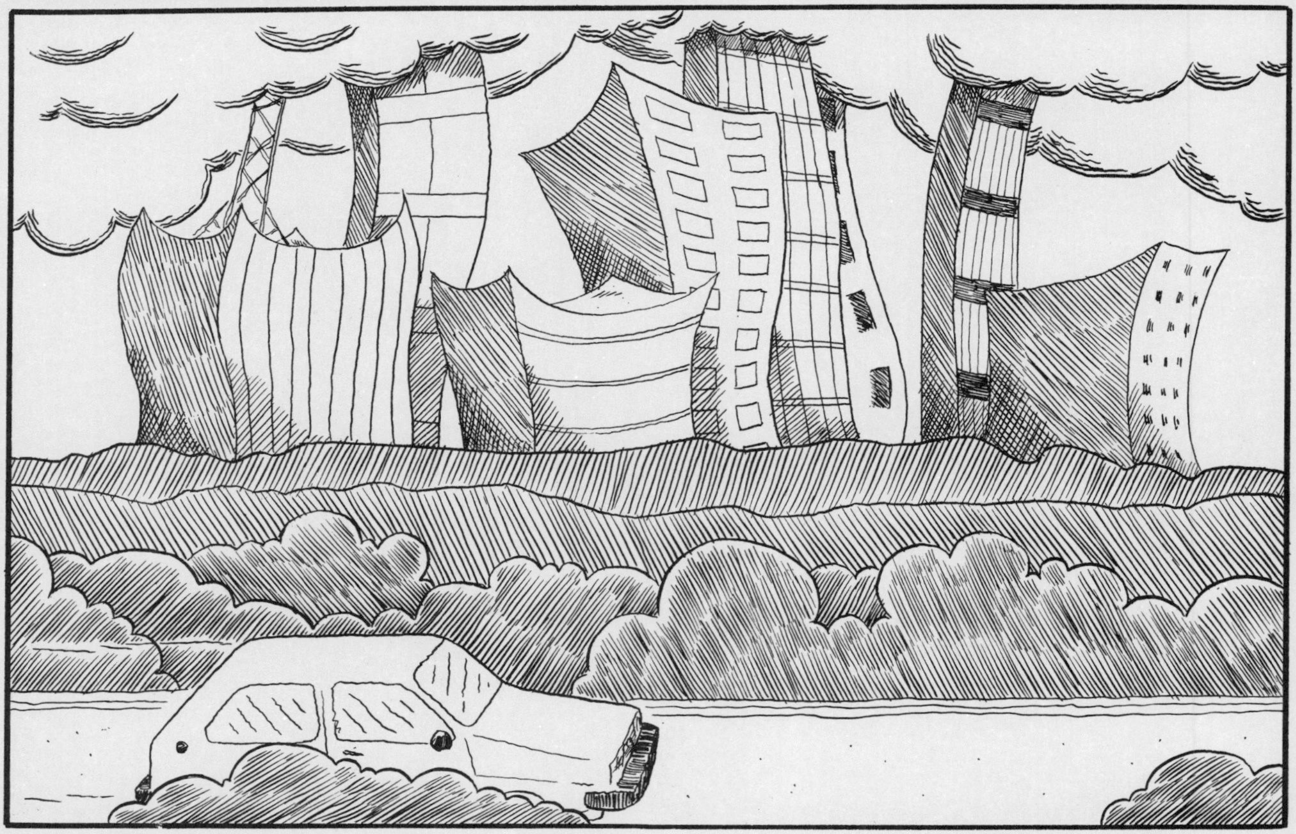

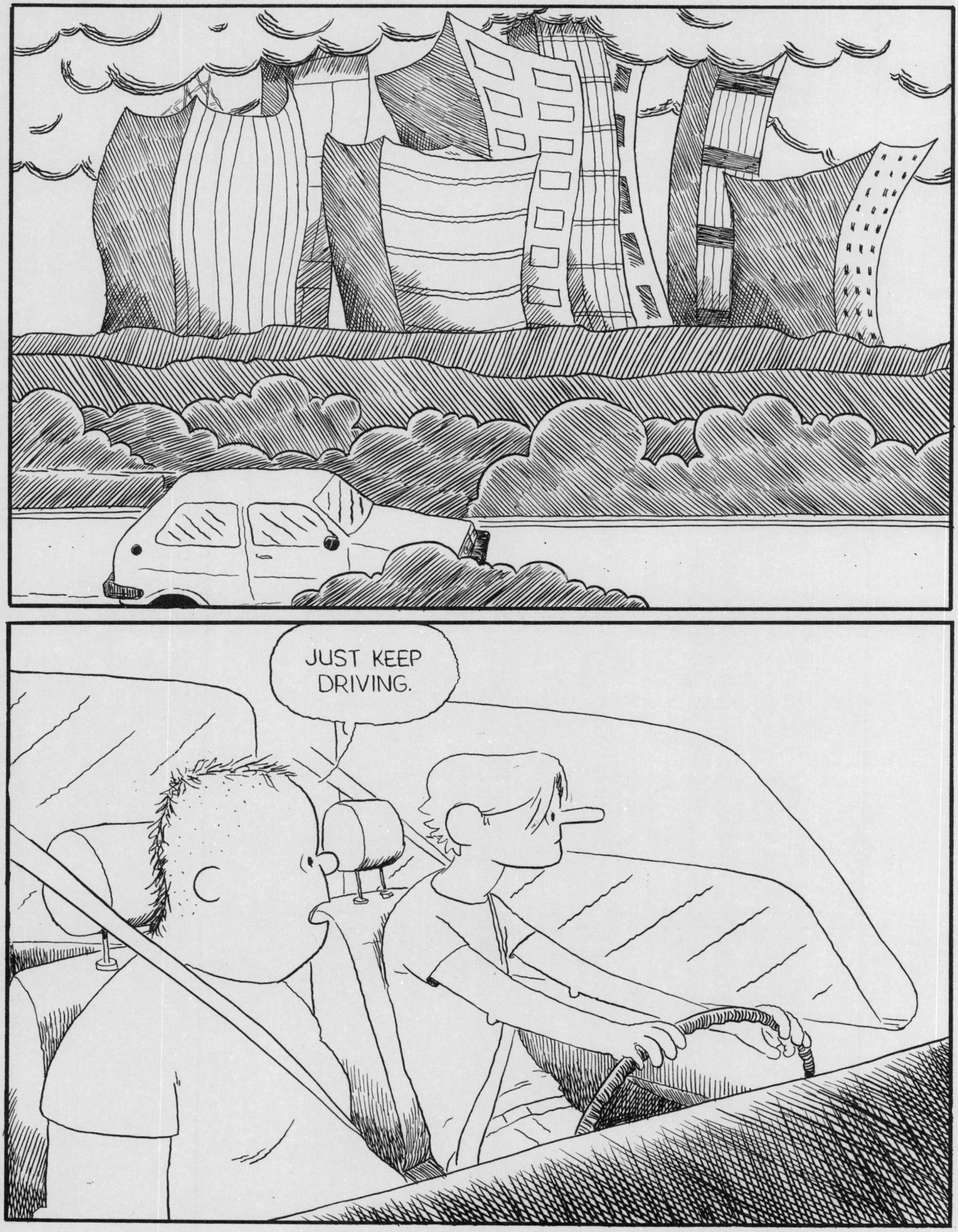
JUST KEEP DRIVING.

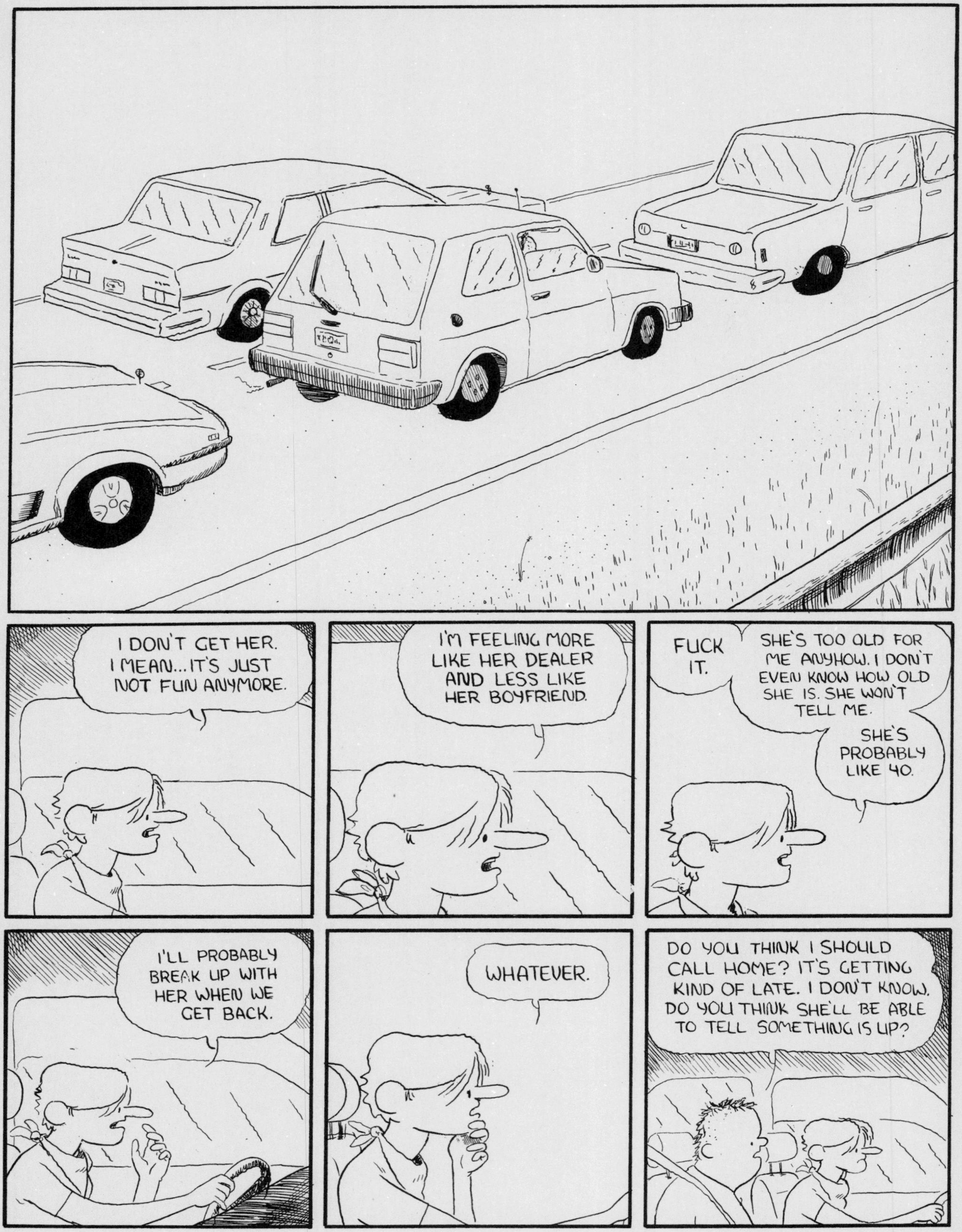
I DON'T GET HER. I MEAN... IT'S JUST NOT FUN ANYMORE.
I'M FEELING MORE LIKE HER DEALER AND LESS LIKE HER BOYFRIEND.
FUCK IT.
SHE'S TOO OLD FOR ME ANYHOW. I DON'T EVEN KNOW HOW OLD SHE IS. SHE WON'T TELL ME.
SHE'S PROBABLY LIKE 40.
I'LL PROBABLY BREAK UP WITH HER WHEN WE GET BACK.
WHATEVER.
DO YOU THINK I SHOULD CALL HOME? IT'S GETTING KIND OF LATE. I DON'T KNOW. DO YOU THINK SHE'LL BE ABLE TO TELL SOMETHING IS UP?

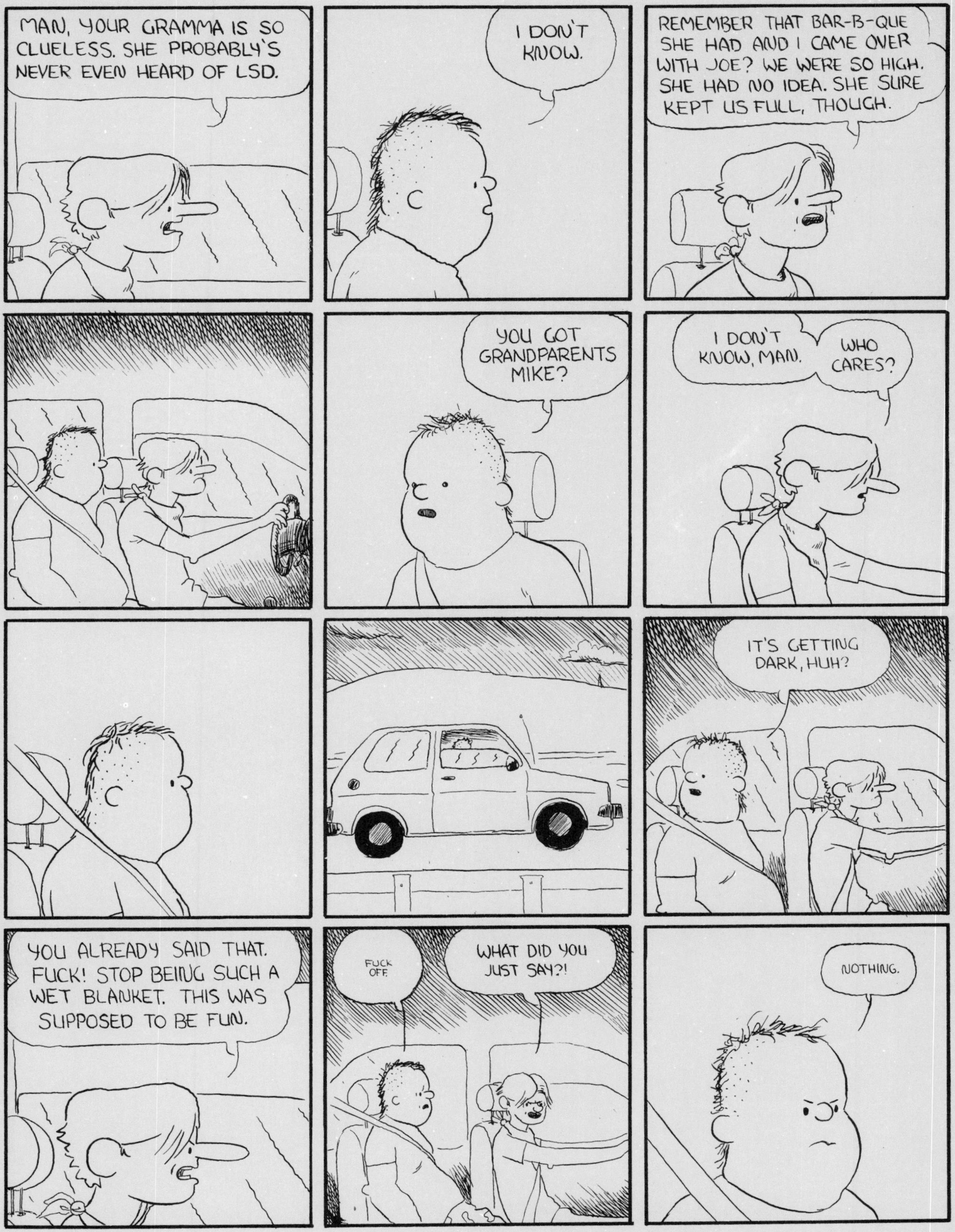
MAN, YOUR GRAMMA IS SO CLUELESS. SHE PROBABLY'S NEVER EVEN HEARD OF LSD.
I DON'T KNOW.
REMEMBER THAT BAR-B-QUE SHE HAD AND I CAME OVER WITH JOE? WE WERE SO HIGH. SHE HAD NO IDEA. SHE SURE KEPT US FULL, THOUGH.
YOU GOT GRANDPARENTS MIKE?
I DON'T KNOW, MAN.
WHO CARES?
IT'S GETTING DARK, HUH?
YOU ALREADY SAID THAT. FUCK! STOP BEING SUCH A WET BLANKET. THIS WAS SUPPOSED TO BE FUN.
FUCK OFF.
WHAT DID YOU JUST SAY?!
NOTHING.

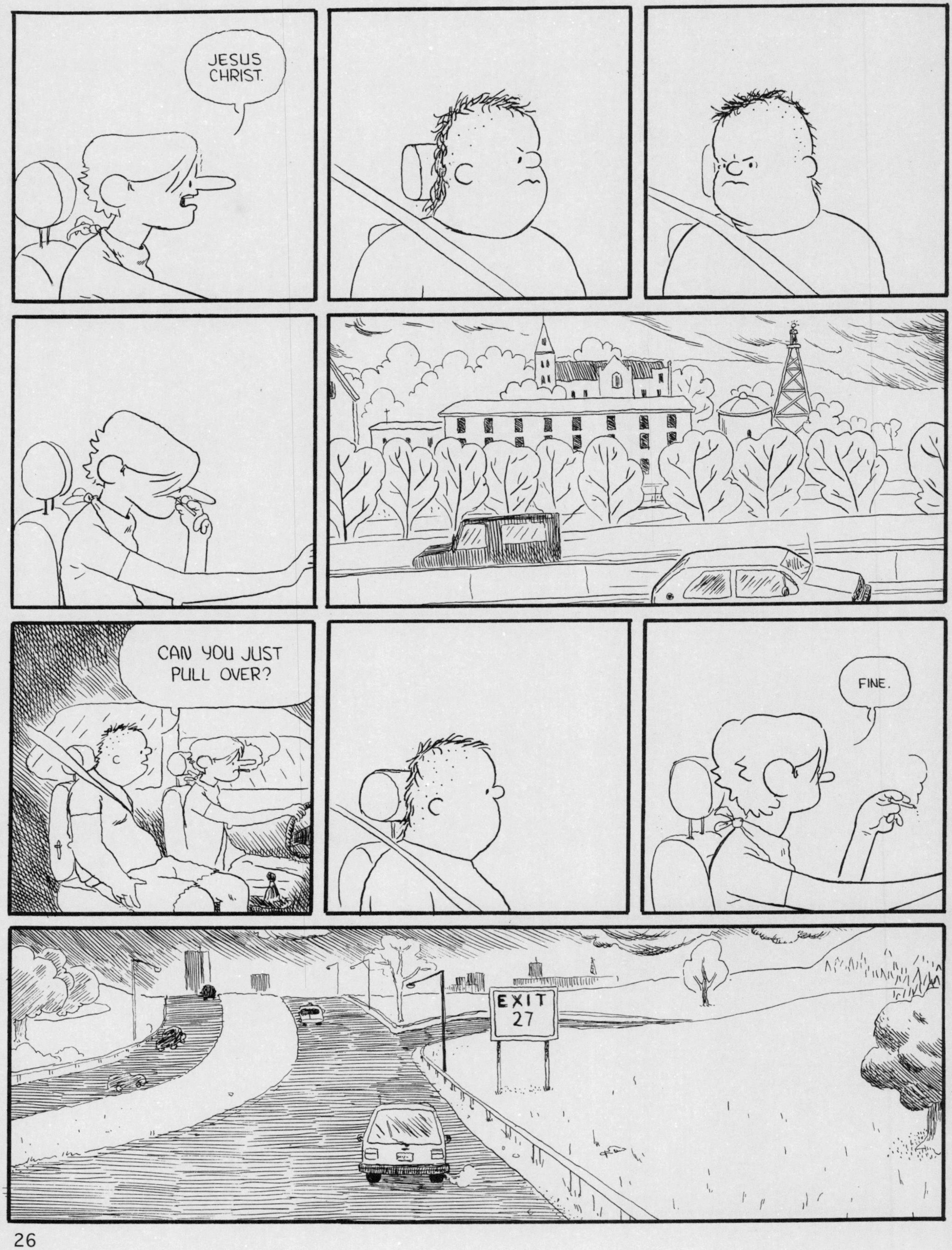
JESUS CHRIST.
CAN YOU JUST PULL OVER?
FINE.
EXIT 27

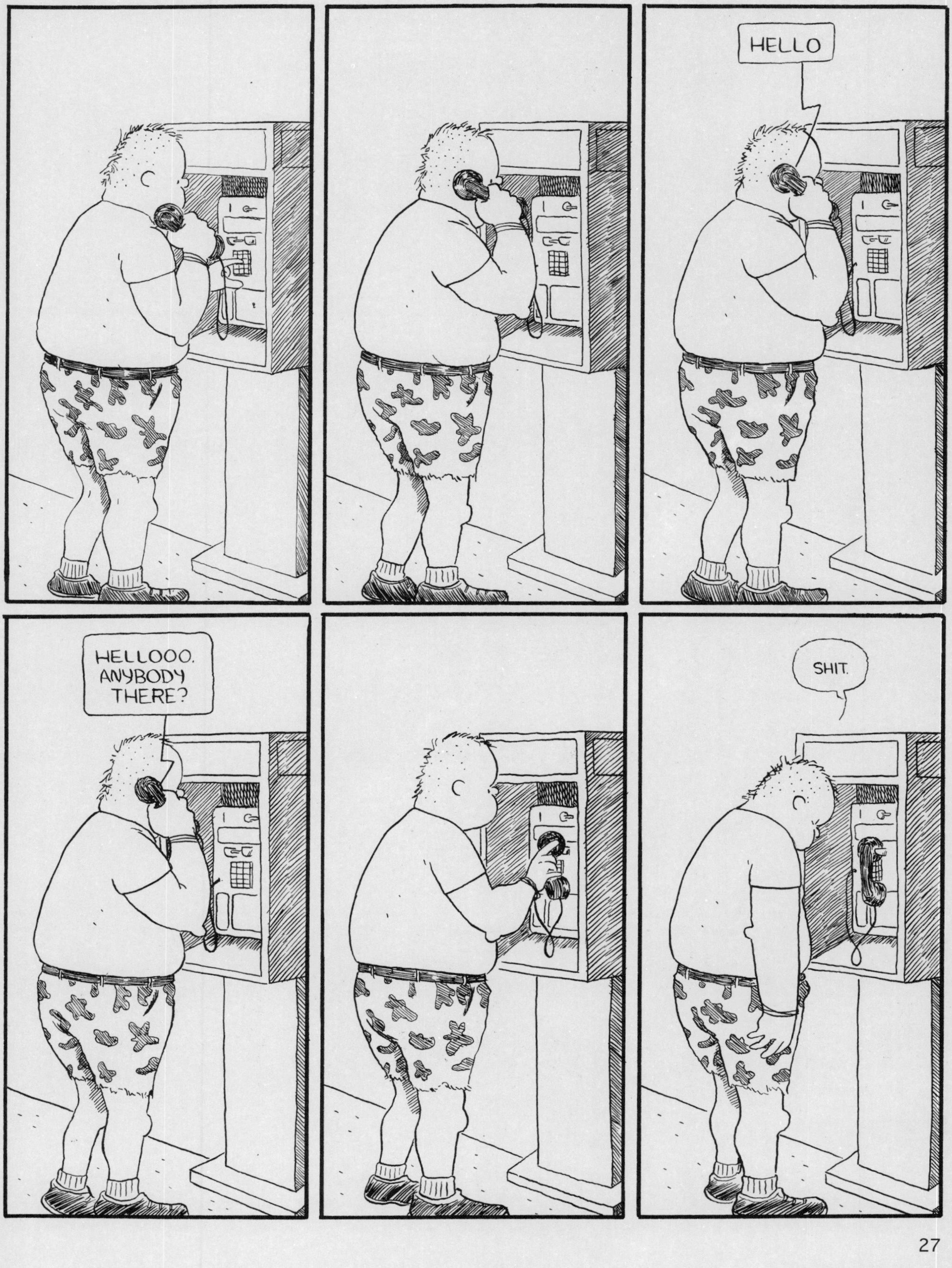
HELLO
HELLOOO. ANYBODY THERE?
SHIT.

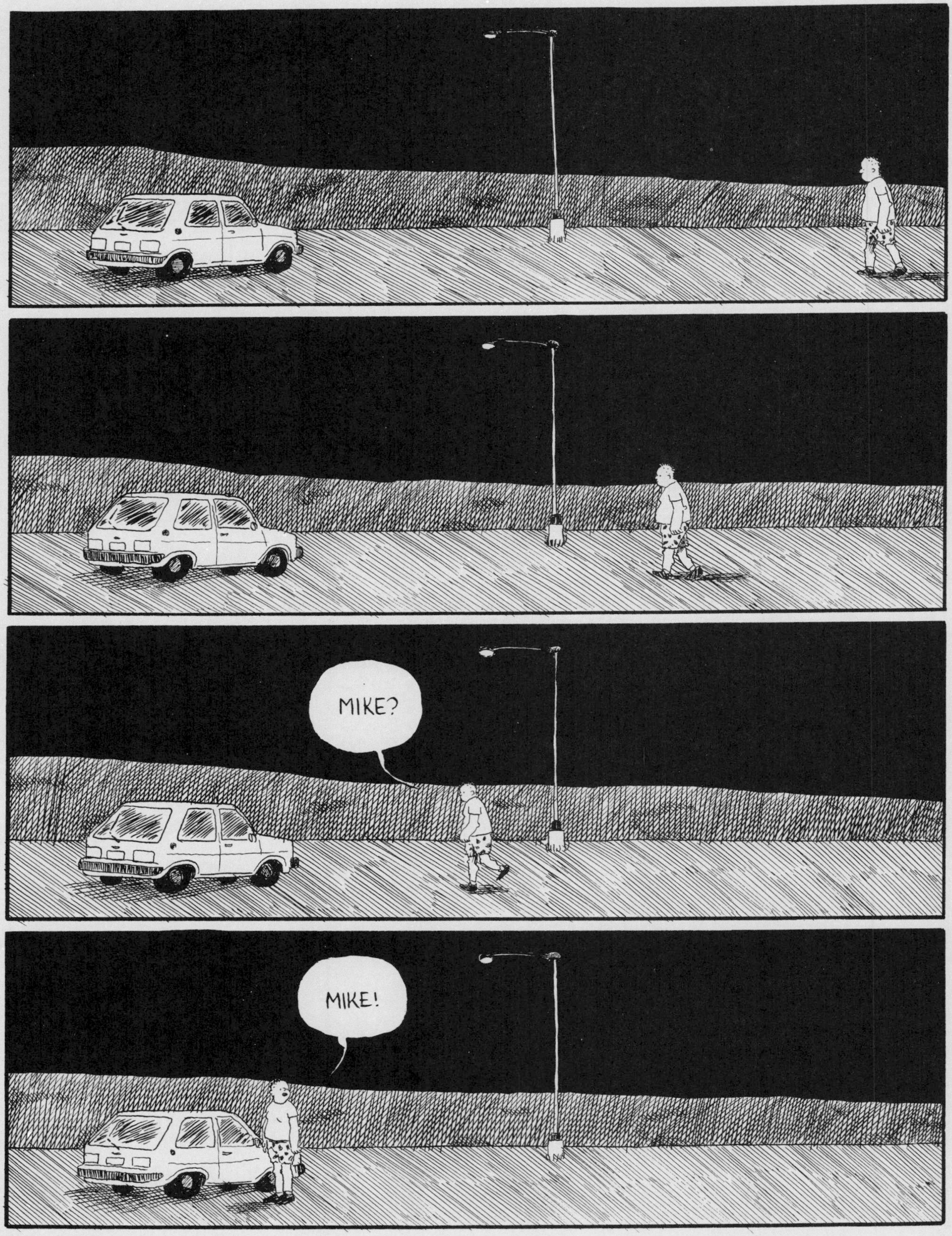
MIKE?
MIKE!

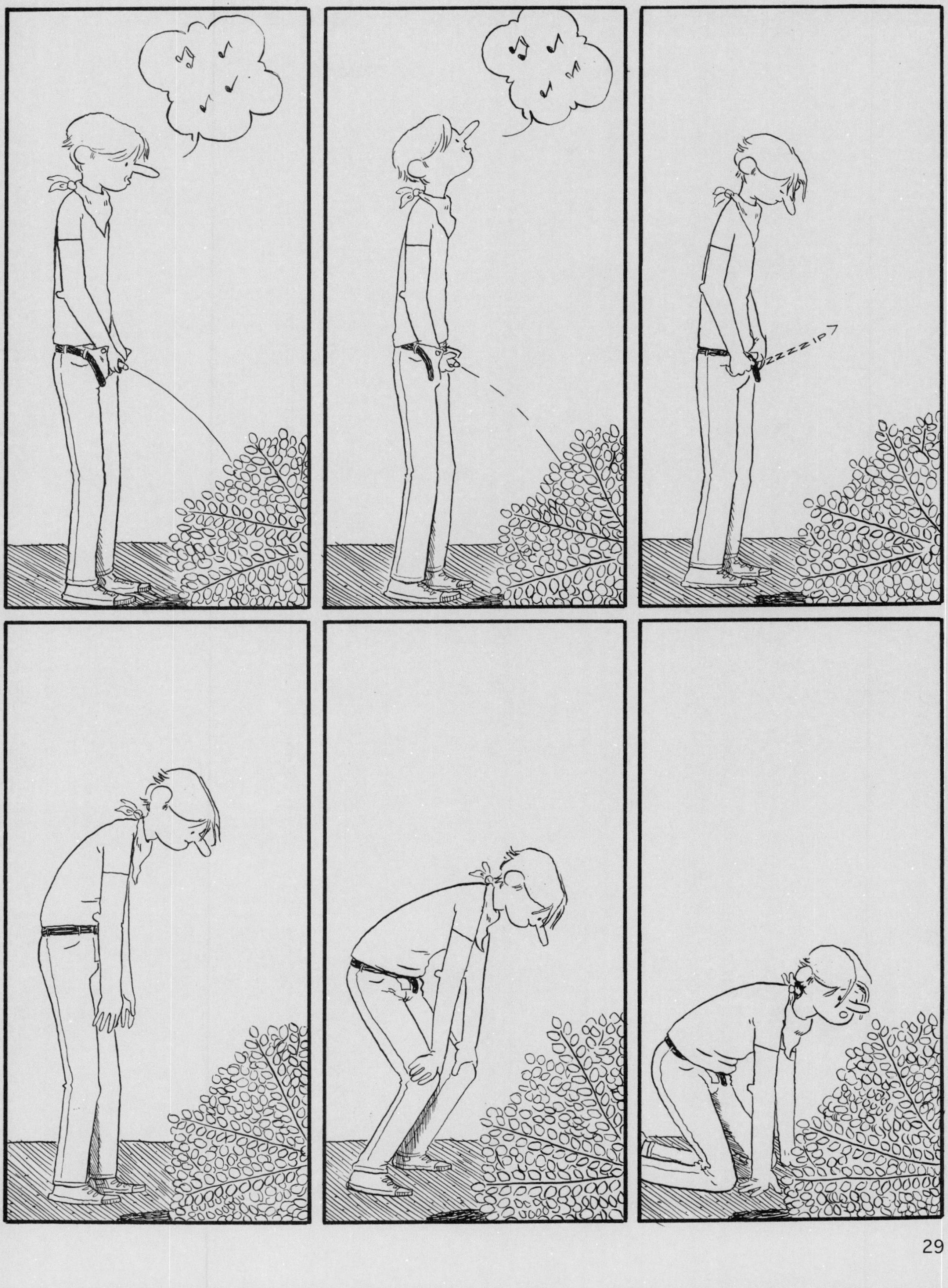
ZZZZZIP

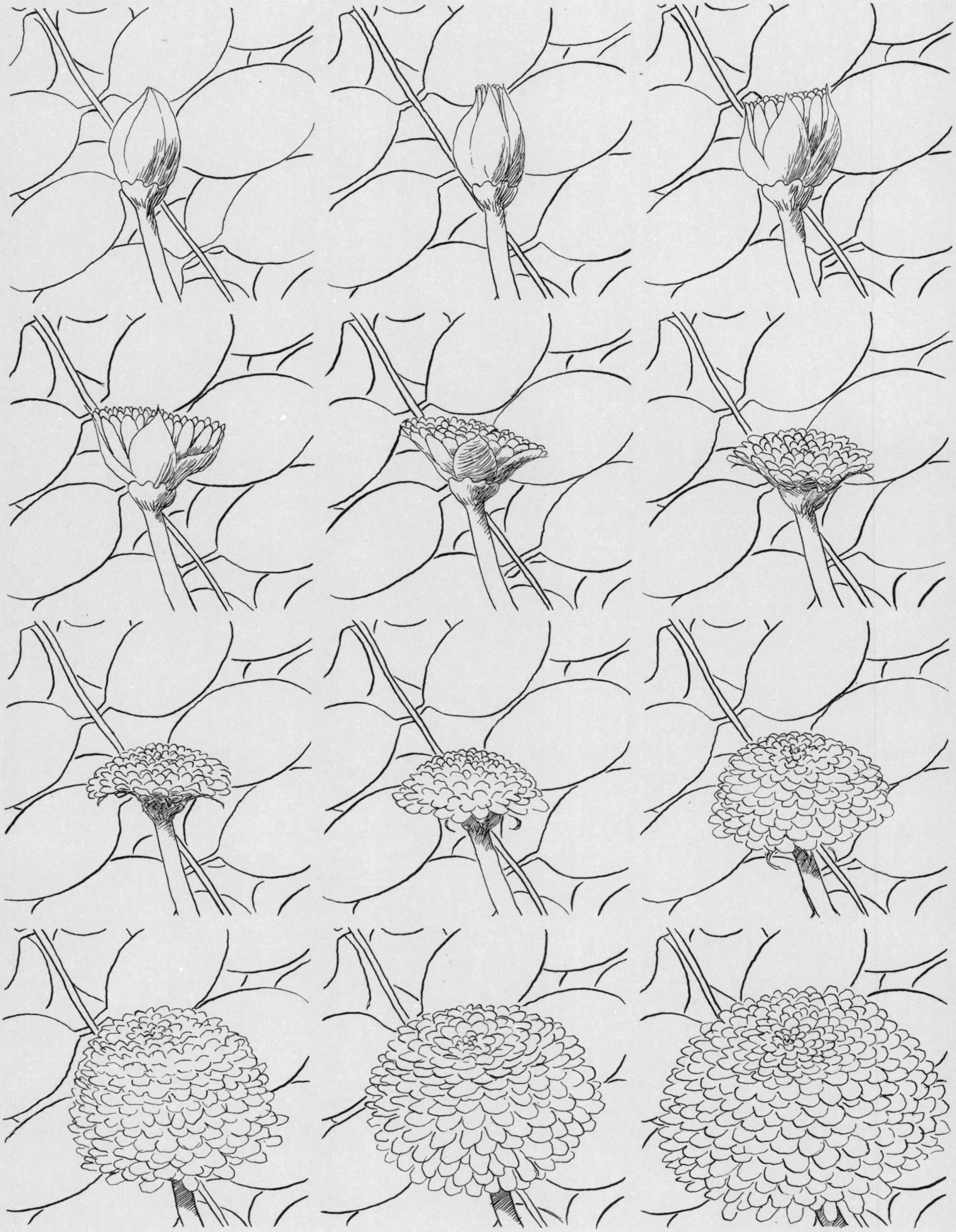

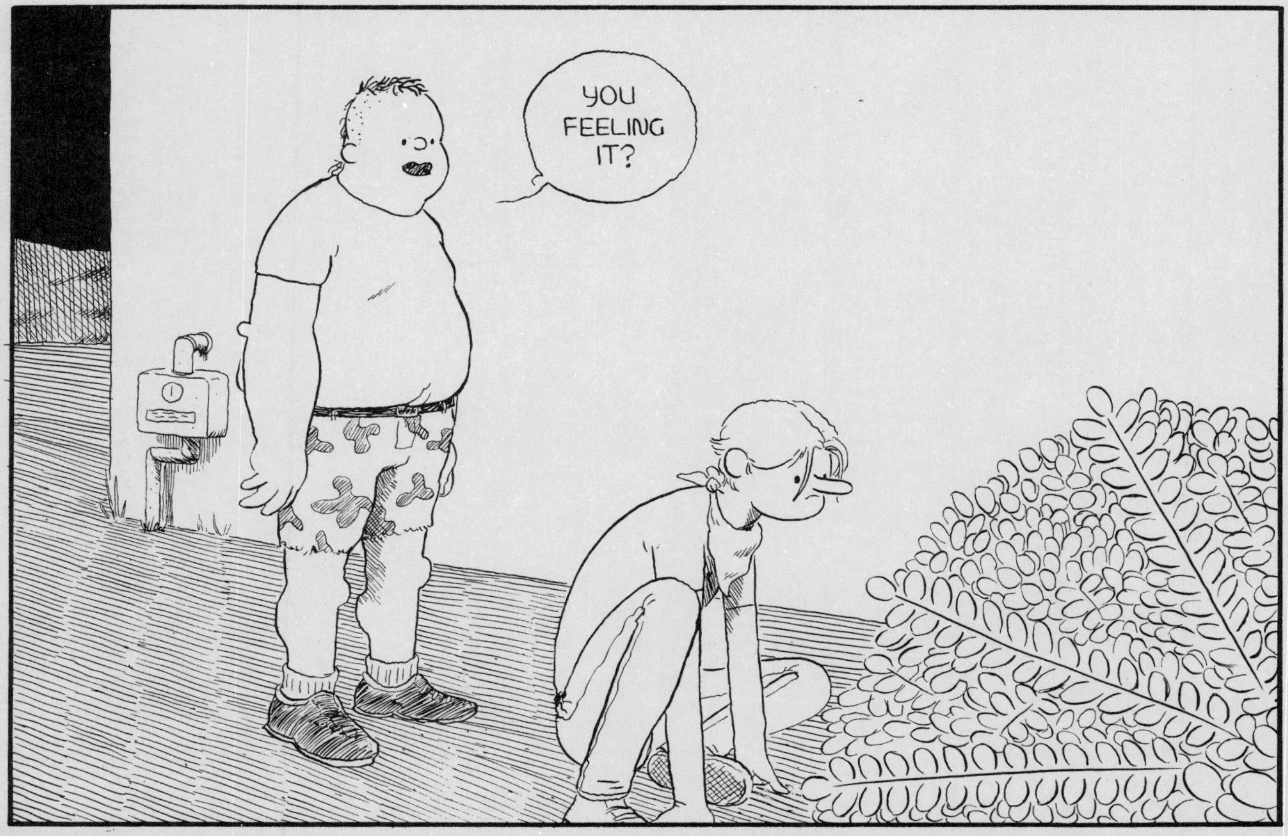
YOU FEELING IT?

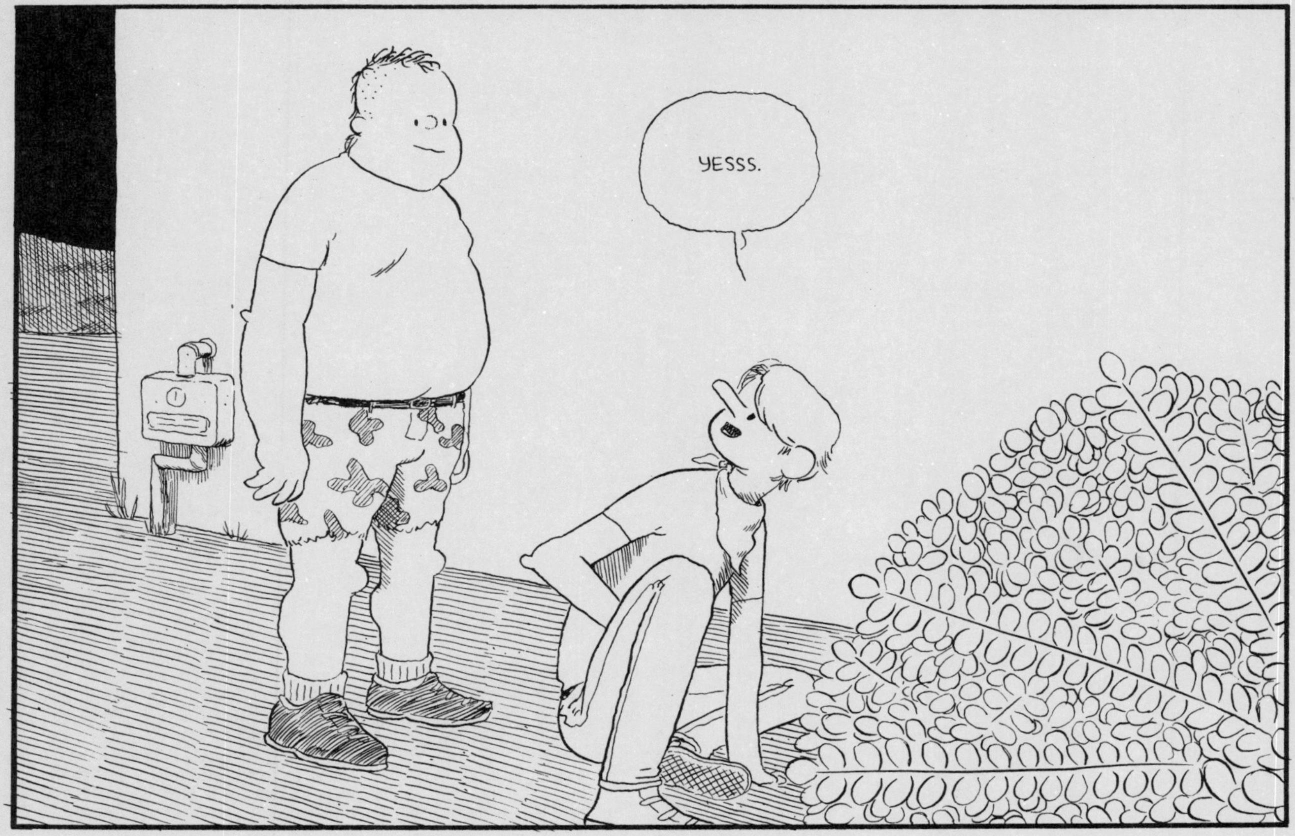
YESSS.

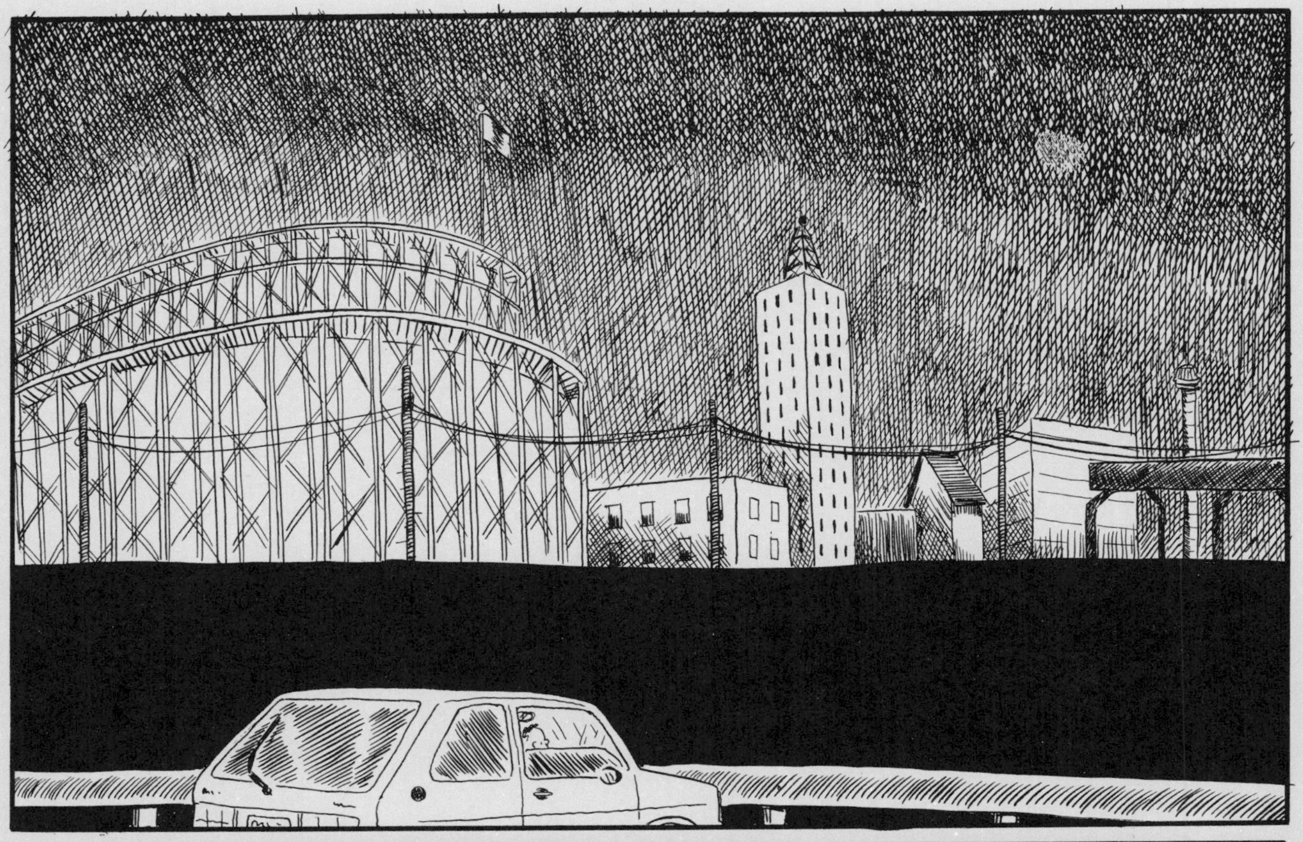

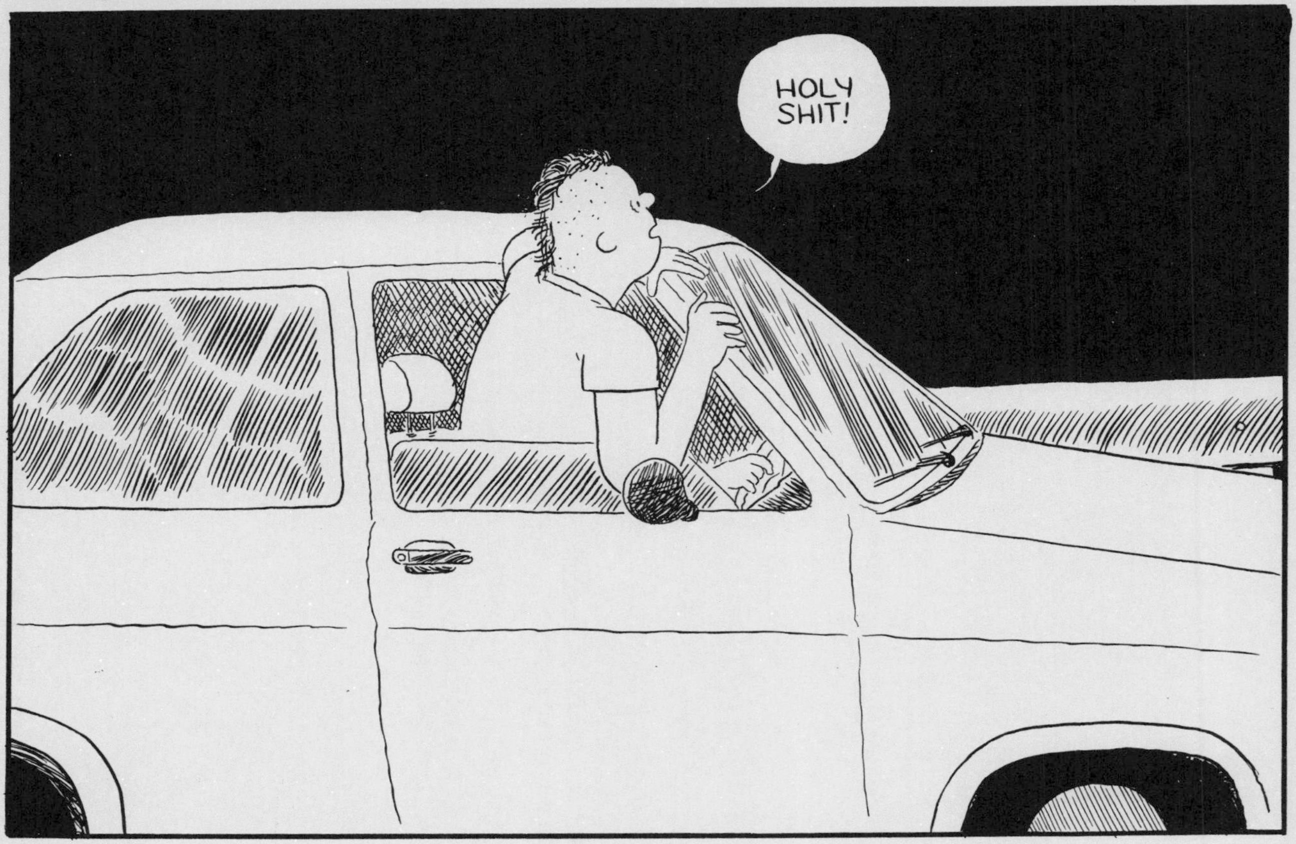
HOLY SHIT!

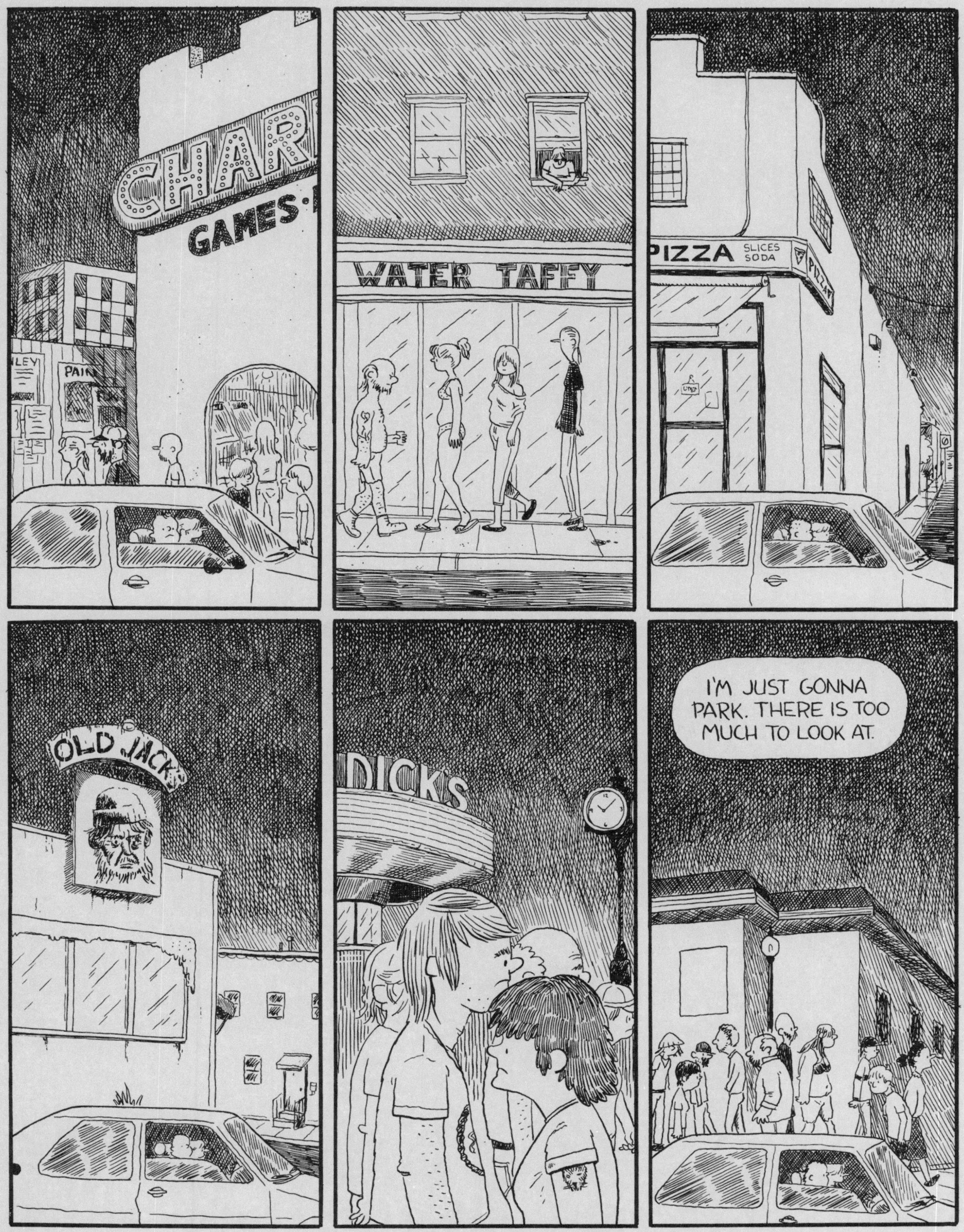
GAMES
WATER TAFFY
PIZZA
SLICES
SODA
OLD JACK'S
DICK'S
I'M JUST GONNA PARK. THERE IS TOO MUCH TO LOOK AT.

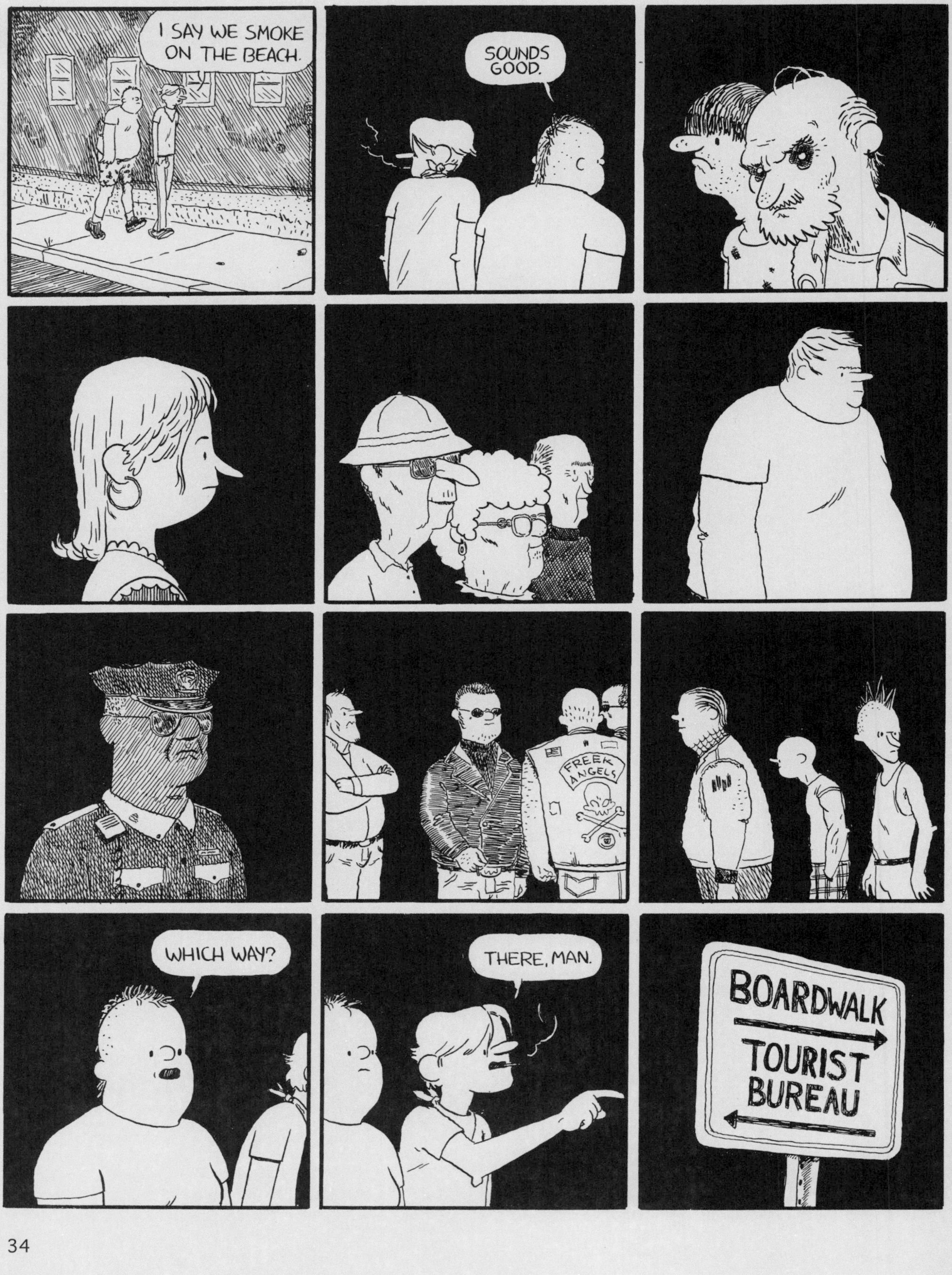
I SAY WE SMOKE ON THE BEACH.
SOUNDS GOOD.
FREEK ANGELS
WHICH WAY?
THERE, MAN.
BOARDWALK
TOURIST BUREAU

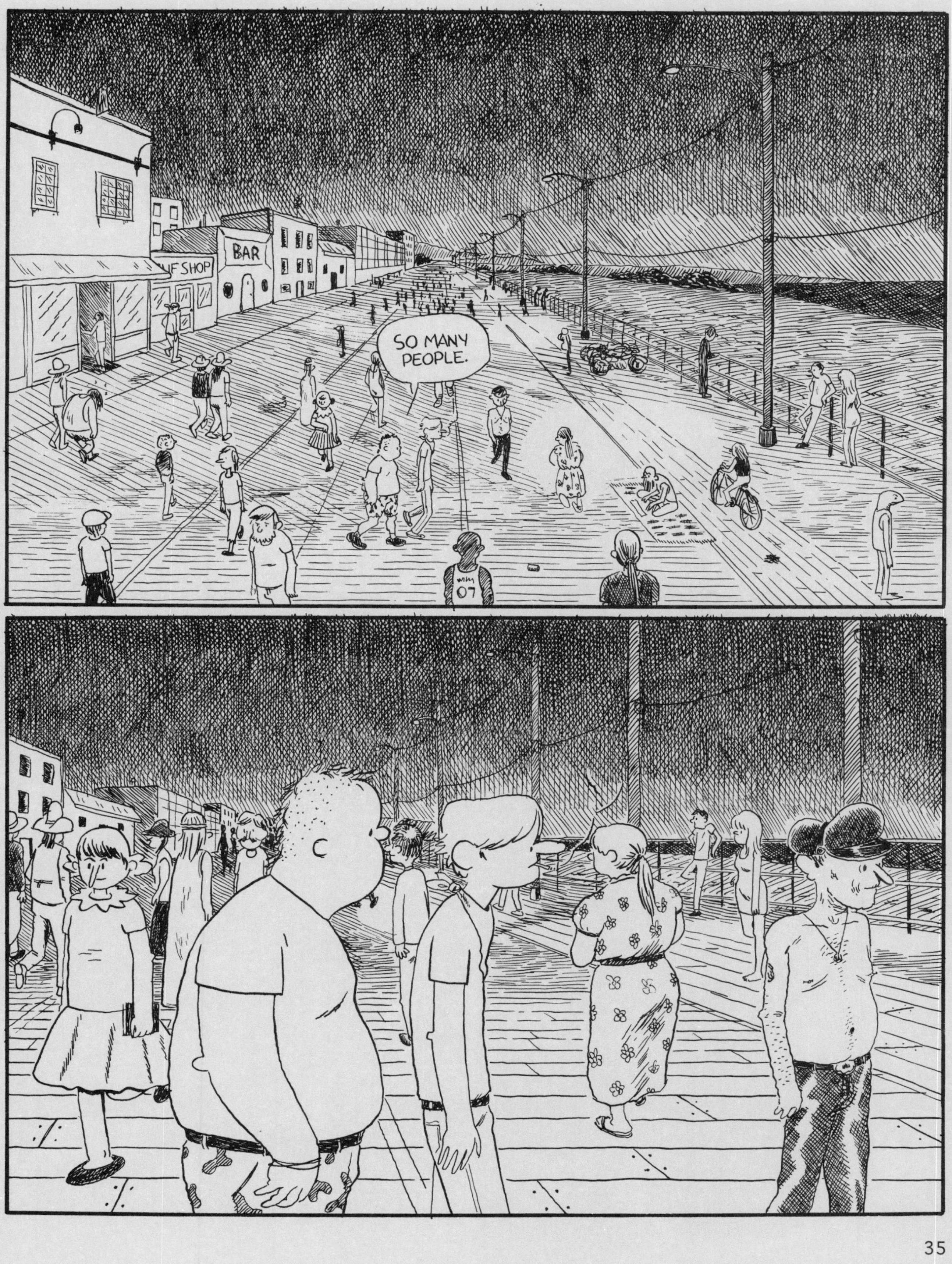

BAR
SURF SHOP
SO MANY PEOPLE.
07

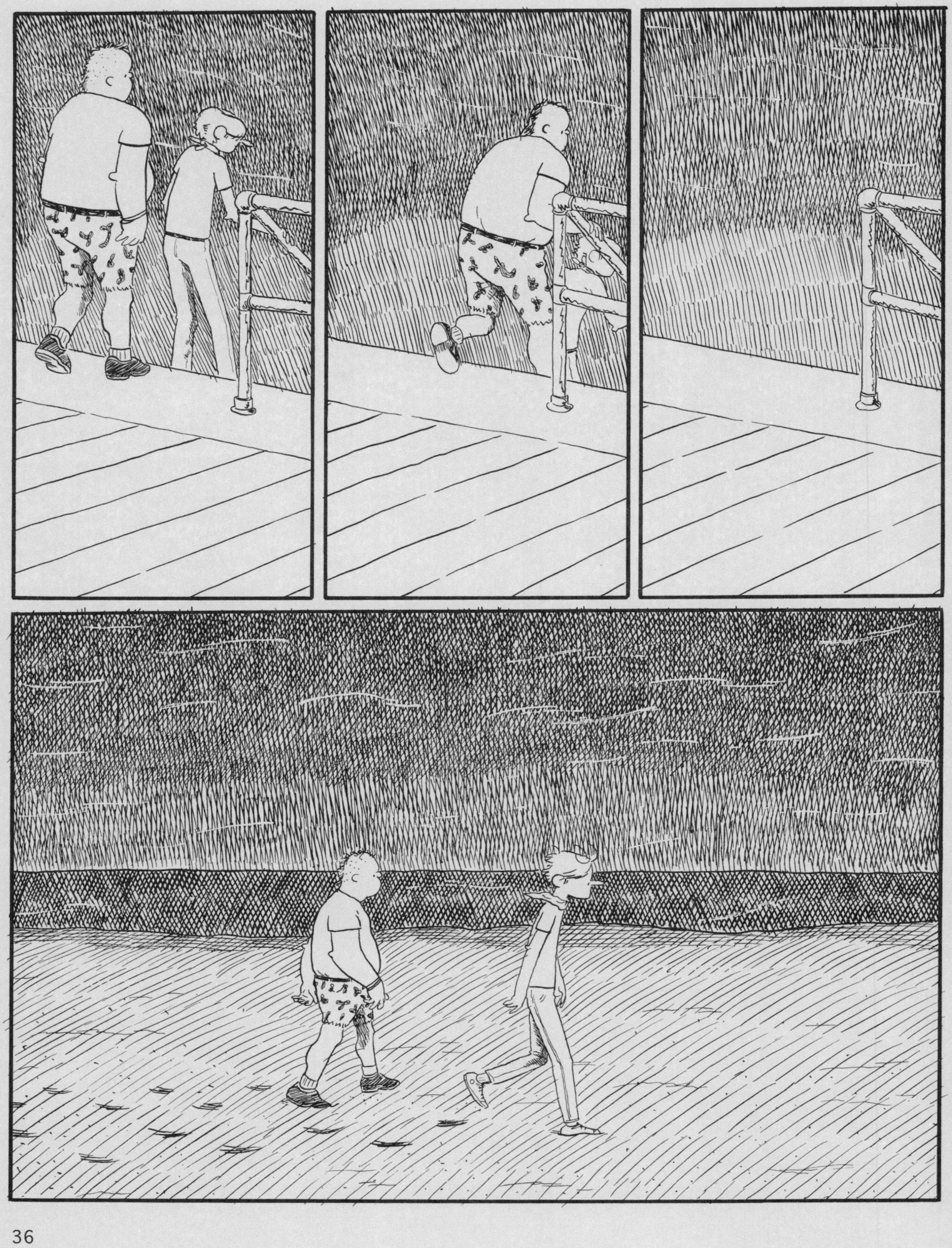

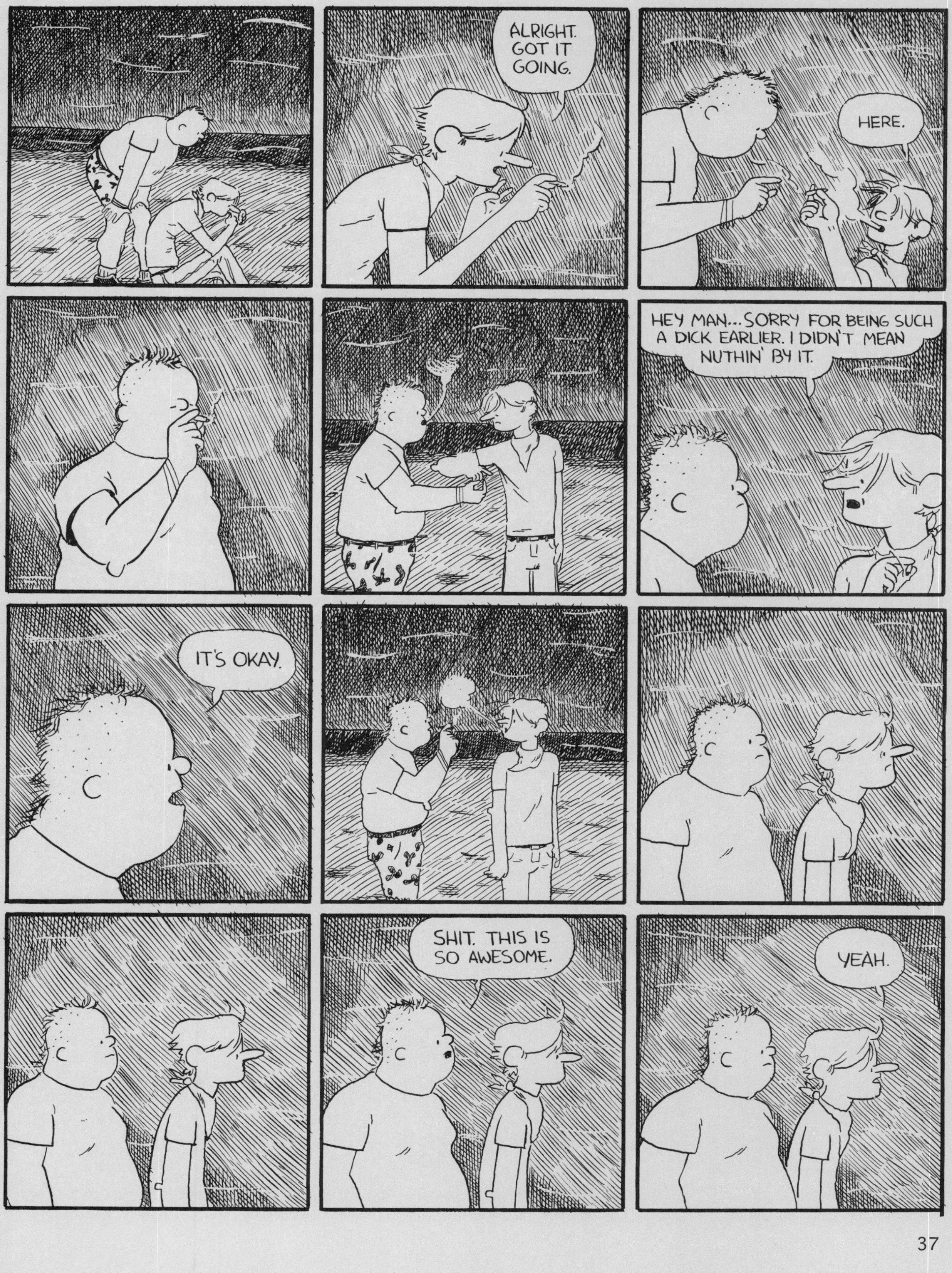
ALRIGHT. GOT IT GOING.
HERE.
HEY MAN... SORRY FOR BEING SUCH A DICK EARLIER. I DIDN'T MEAN NUTHIN' BY IT.
IT'S OKAY.
SHIT. THIS IS SO AWESOME.
YEAH.

MY FRIEND JENNY
SAID ONCE THAT I HAVE
A CALMING PRESENCE.

MAYBE IT'S BECAUSE
I AM SO QUIET.

DOGS AND CATS
ALWAYS SEEM RELAXED
AROUND ME.

EVEN THE CRAZY ONES.

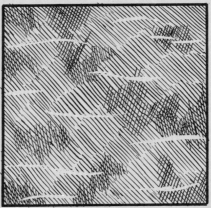

I DON'T KNOW.

I'M A PRETTY
NERVOUS GUY ON
THE INSIDE.

I THINK JENNY ONLY
TALKS TO ME BECAUSE
WE WORK TOGETHER.

IT'S NOT LIKE WE
HANG OUT AFTER
WORK.

MOST OF MY LIFE
I'VE HAD A SMALL
GROUP OF FRIENDS.

PEOPLE MAKE
ME NERVOUS.

THEY TAKE A
LOT OUT OF ME.

I'VE ALWAYS BEEN BIG. IN ELEMENTARY SCHOOL I WOULD ALWAYS HURT THE OTHER KIDS.

MOM SAID IT WAS JUST THAT I DIDN'T KNOW MY OWN STRENGTH.

I PRETTY MUCH QUIT PLAYING AT RECESS AFTER I ACCIDENTALLY BROKE TOM MILLER'S ARM DURING A FOOTBALL GAME.

AFTER THAT I GOT REALLY QUIET.

IT FELT SAFER JUST TO WATCH.

THIS WAS ABOUT THE TIME THAT MOM STARTED TO PULL AWAY.

I STILL FEEL PARALYZED WHEN I THINK ABOUT TOM'S STUPID BROKEN ARM.

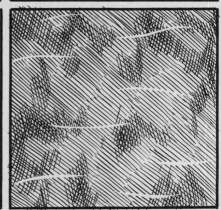

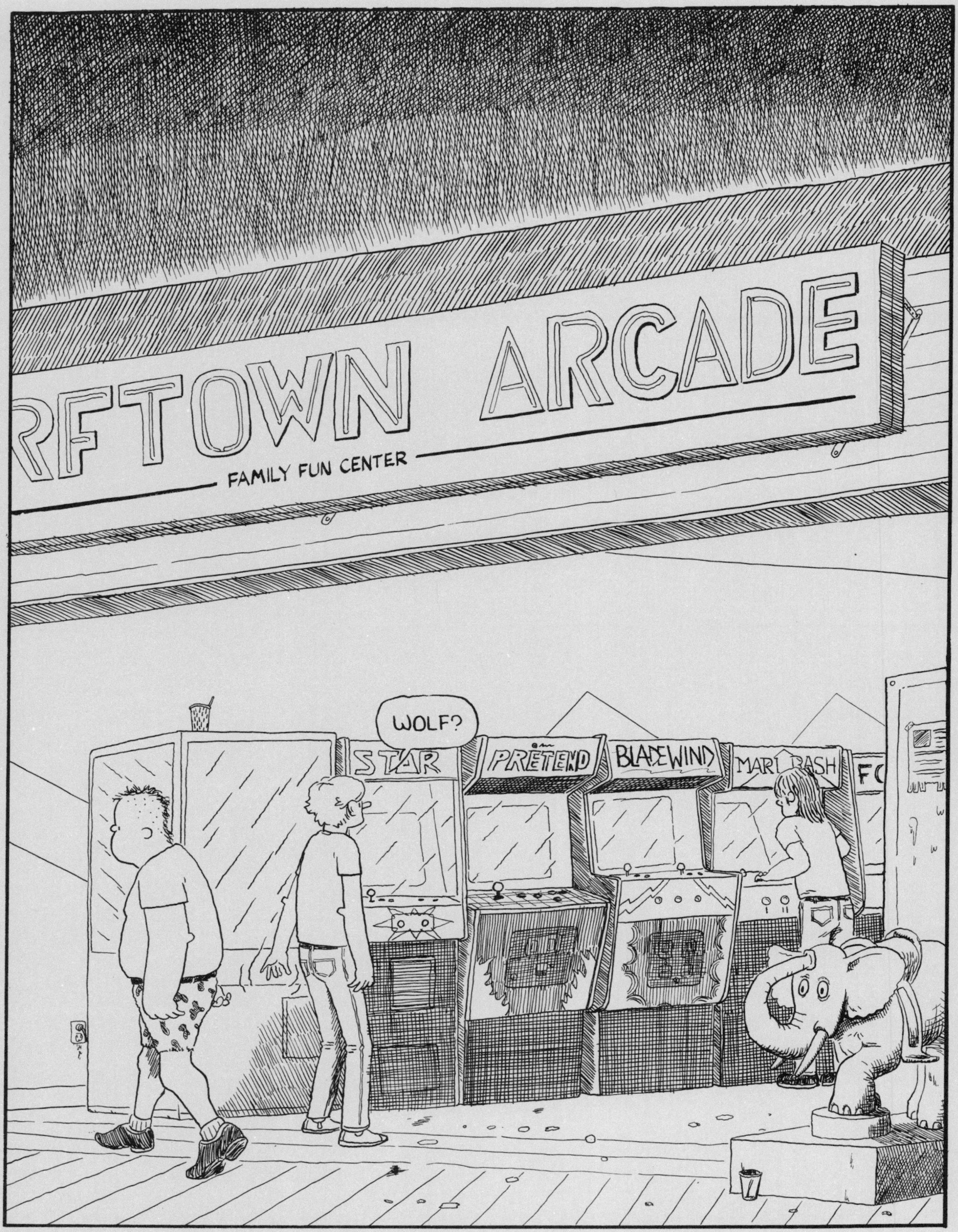
RFTOWN ARCADE
FAMILY FUN CENTER
WOLF?
STAR
PRETEND
BLADEWIND
MARL BASH
FO

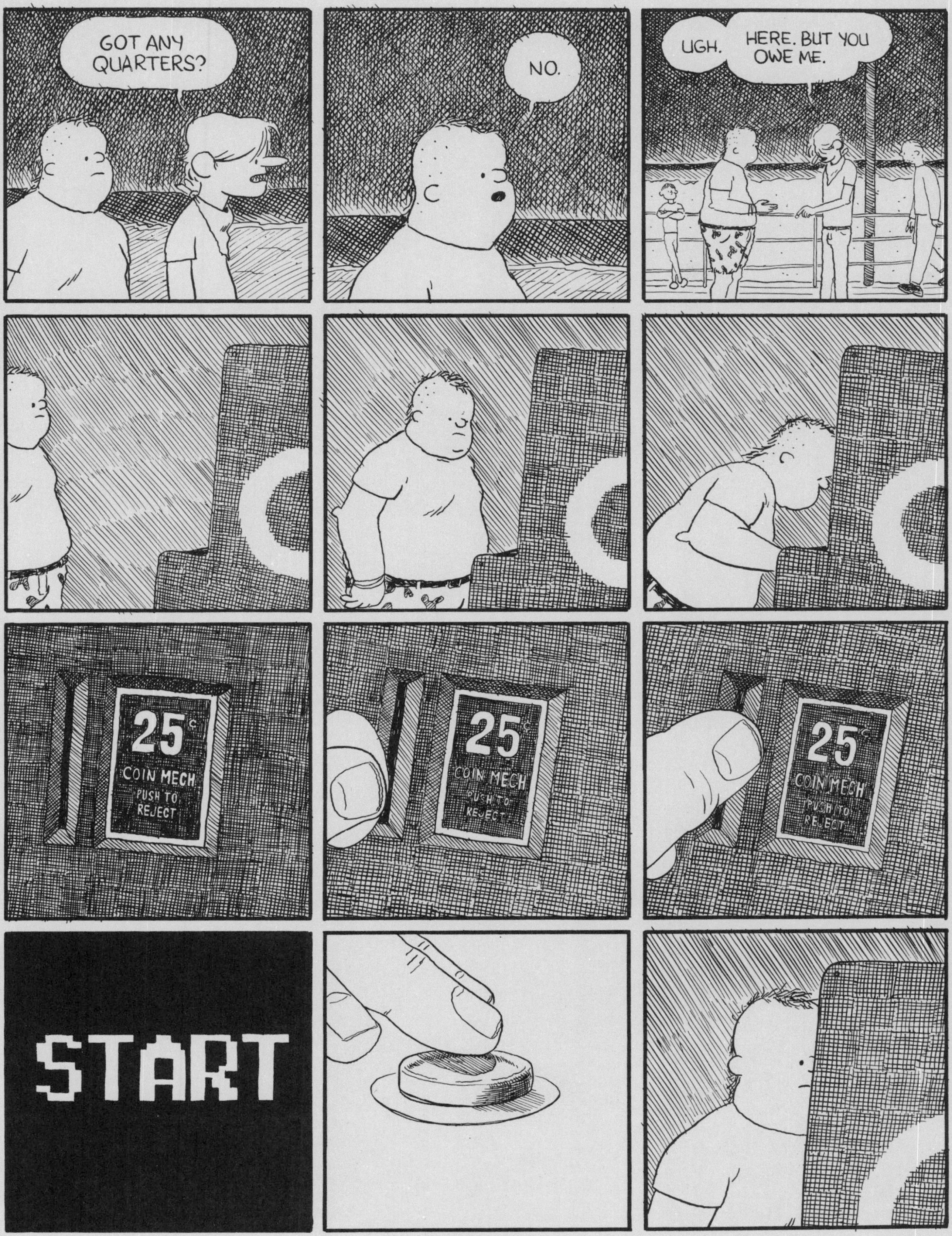
GOT ANY QUARTERS?
NO.
UGH.
HERE. BUT YOU OWE ME.
25¢
COIN MECH
PUSH TO REJECT
25¢
COIN MECH
PUSH TO REJECT
25¢
COIN MECH
PUSH TO REJECT
START

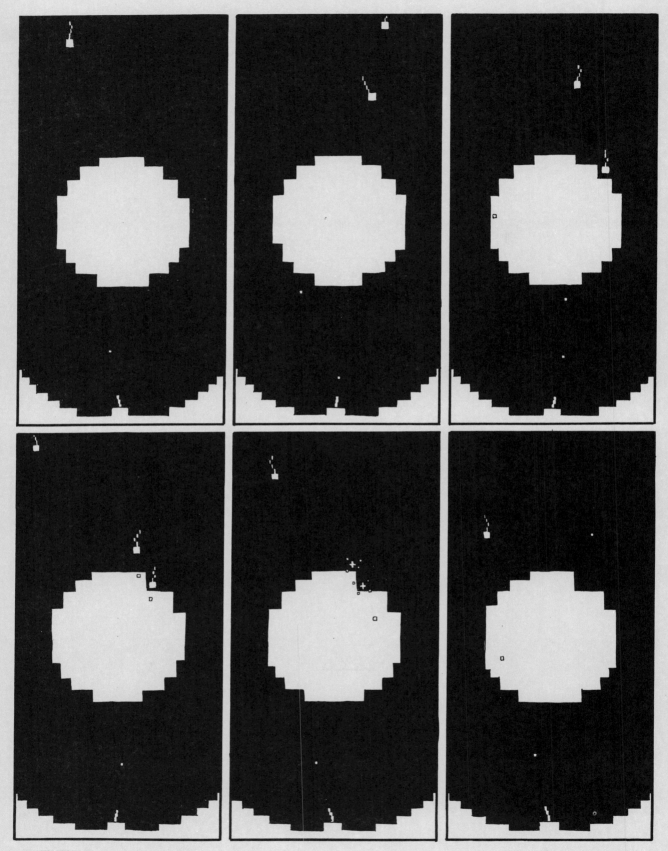

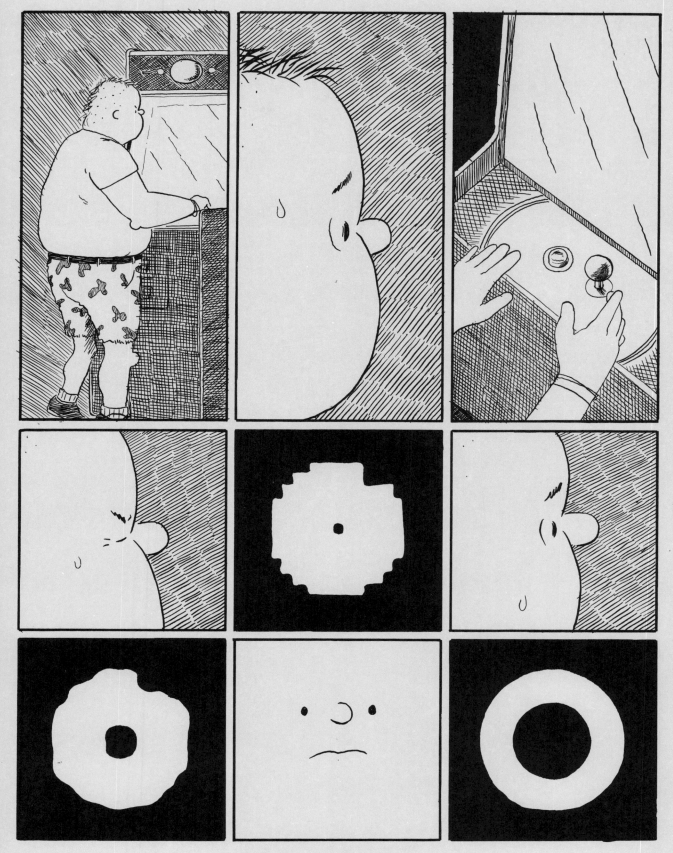

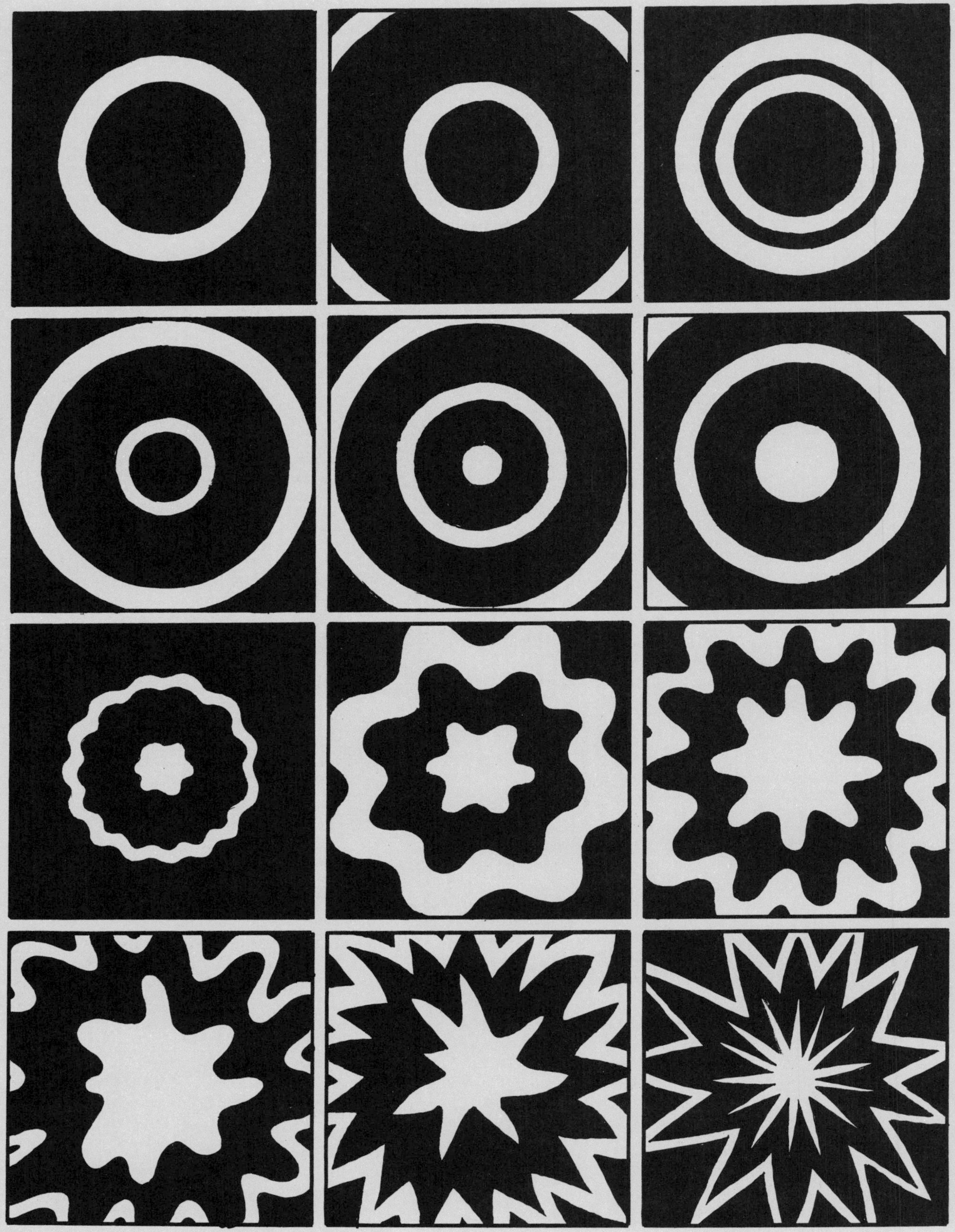

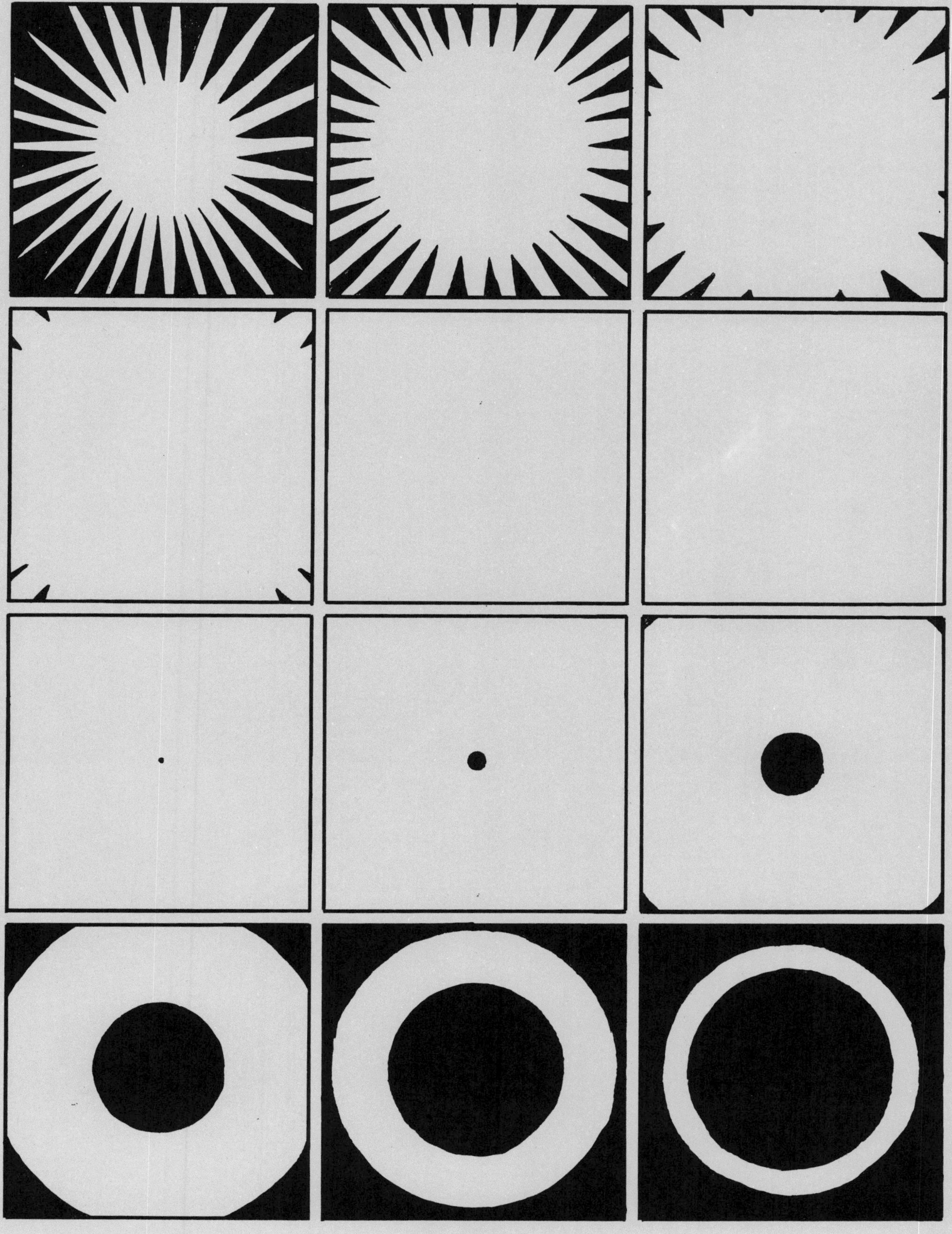

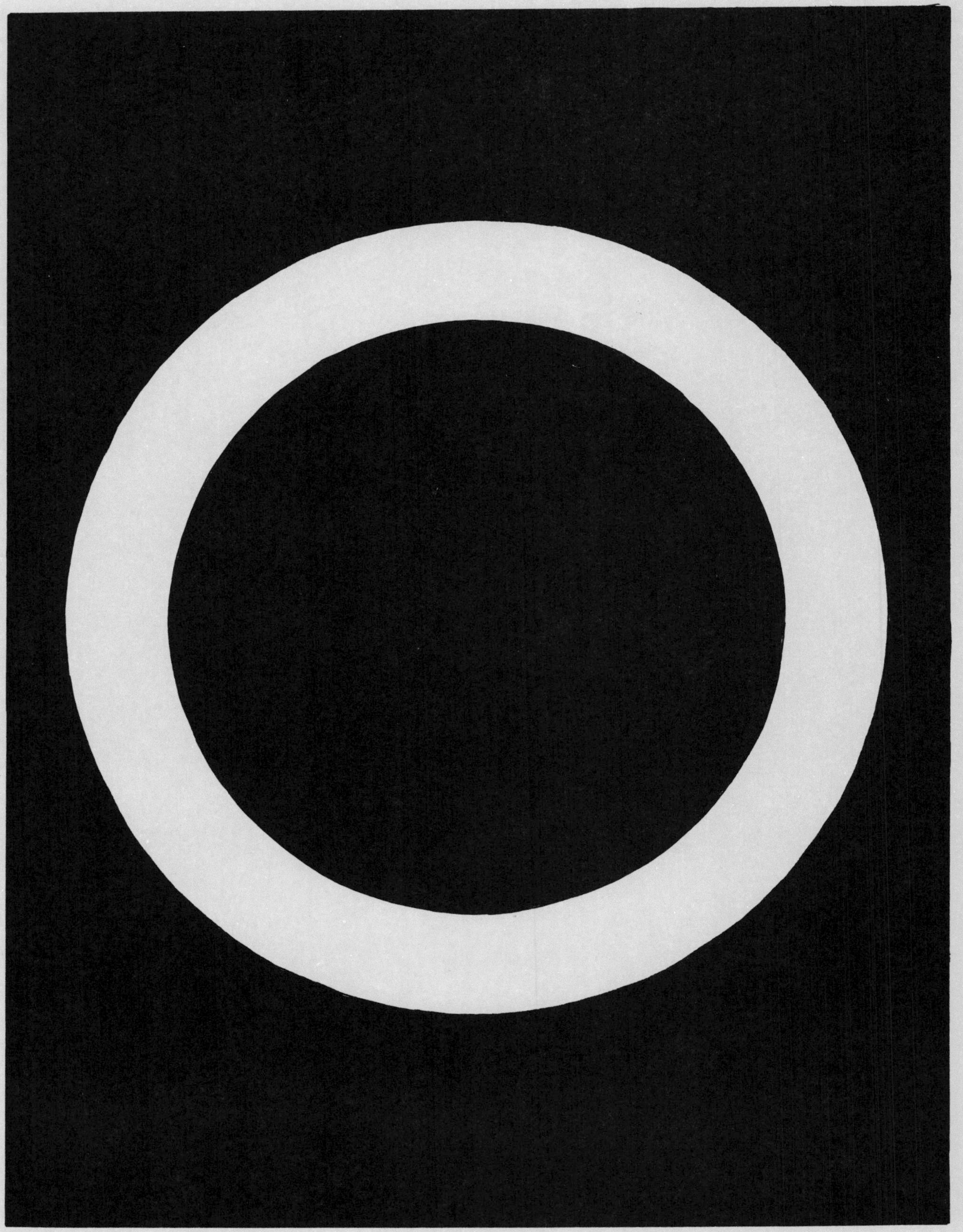

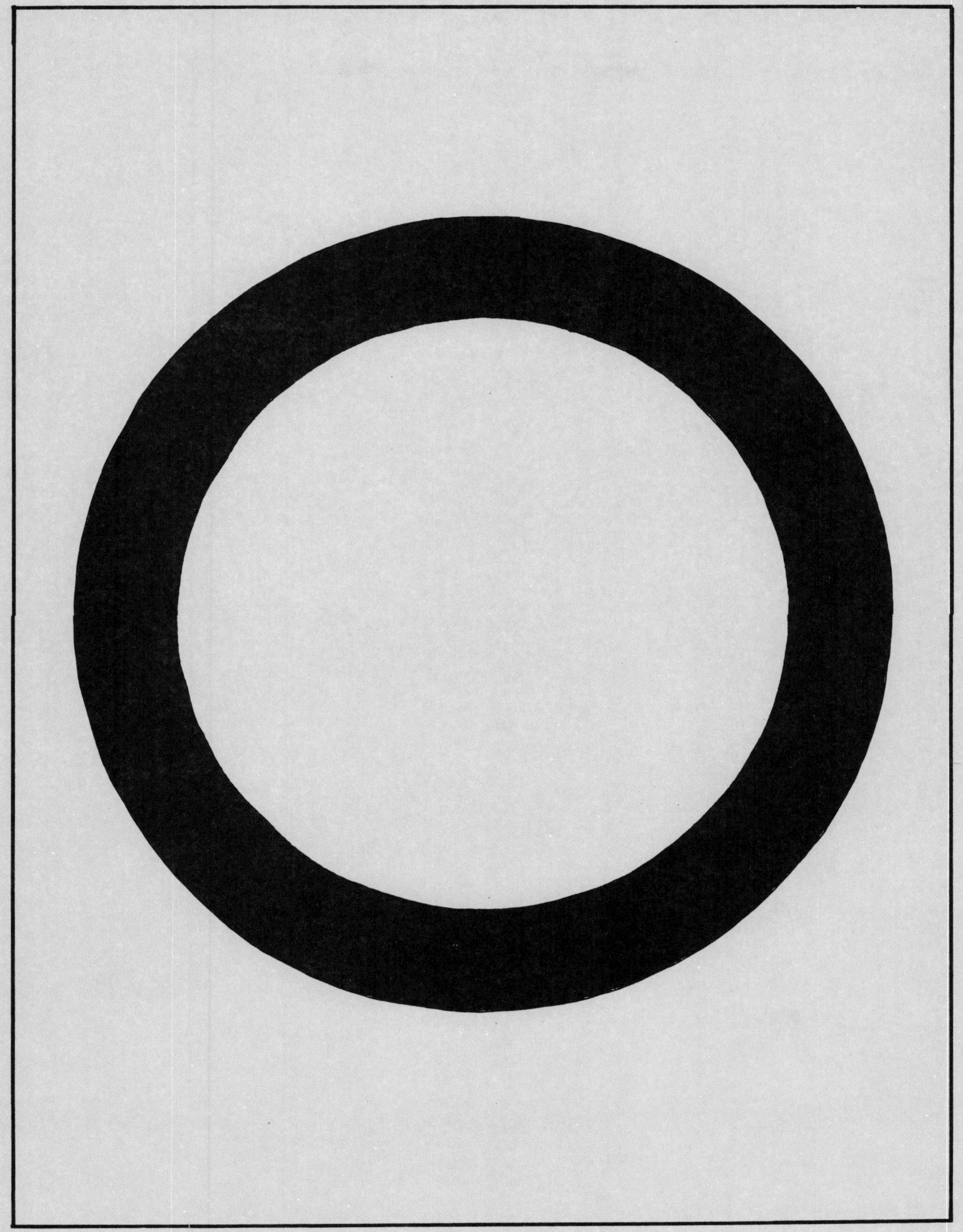

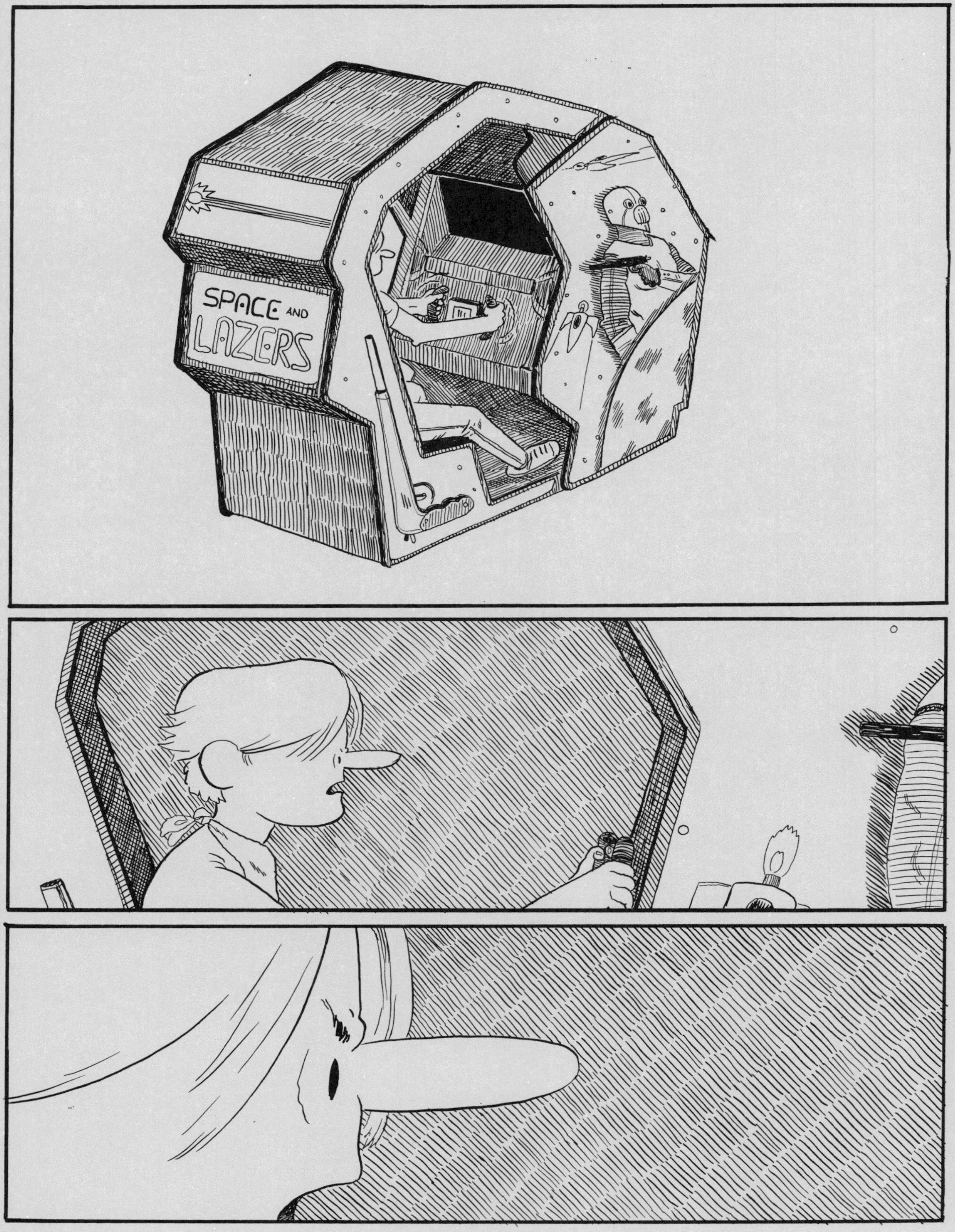
SPACE AND
LAZERS

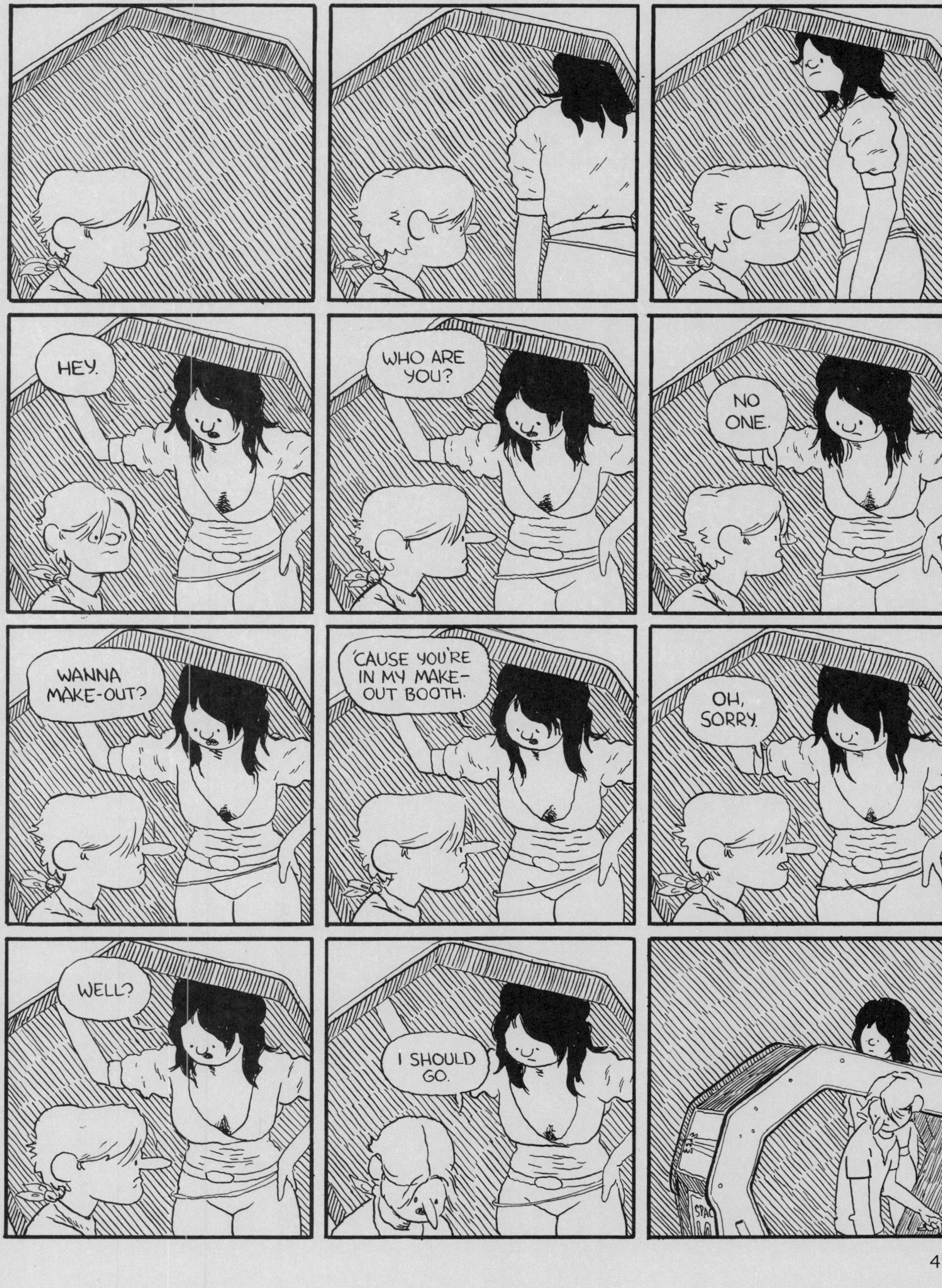
HEY.
WHO ARE YOU?
NO ONE.
WANNA MAKE-OUT?
'CAUSE YOU'RE IN MY MAKE-OUT BOOTH.
OH, SORRY.
WELL?
I SHOULD GO.

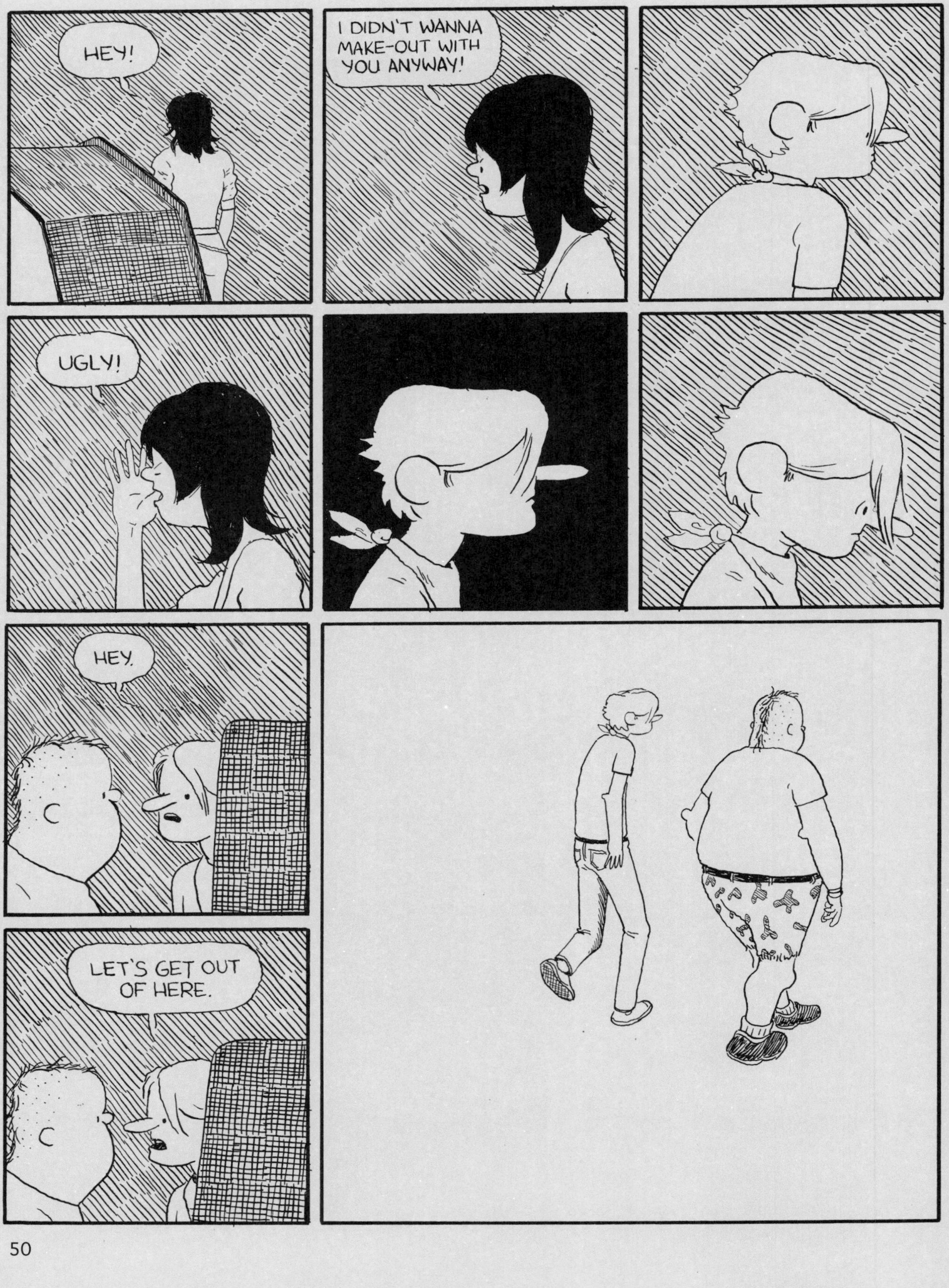
HEY!
I DIDN'T WANNA MAKE-OUT WITH YOU ANYWAY!
UGLY!
HEY.
LET'S GET OUT OF HERE.

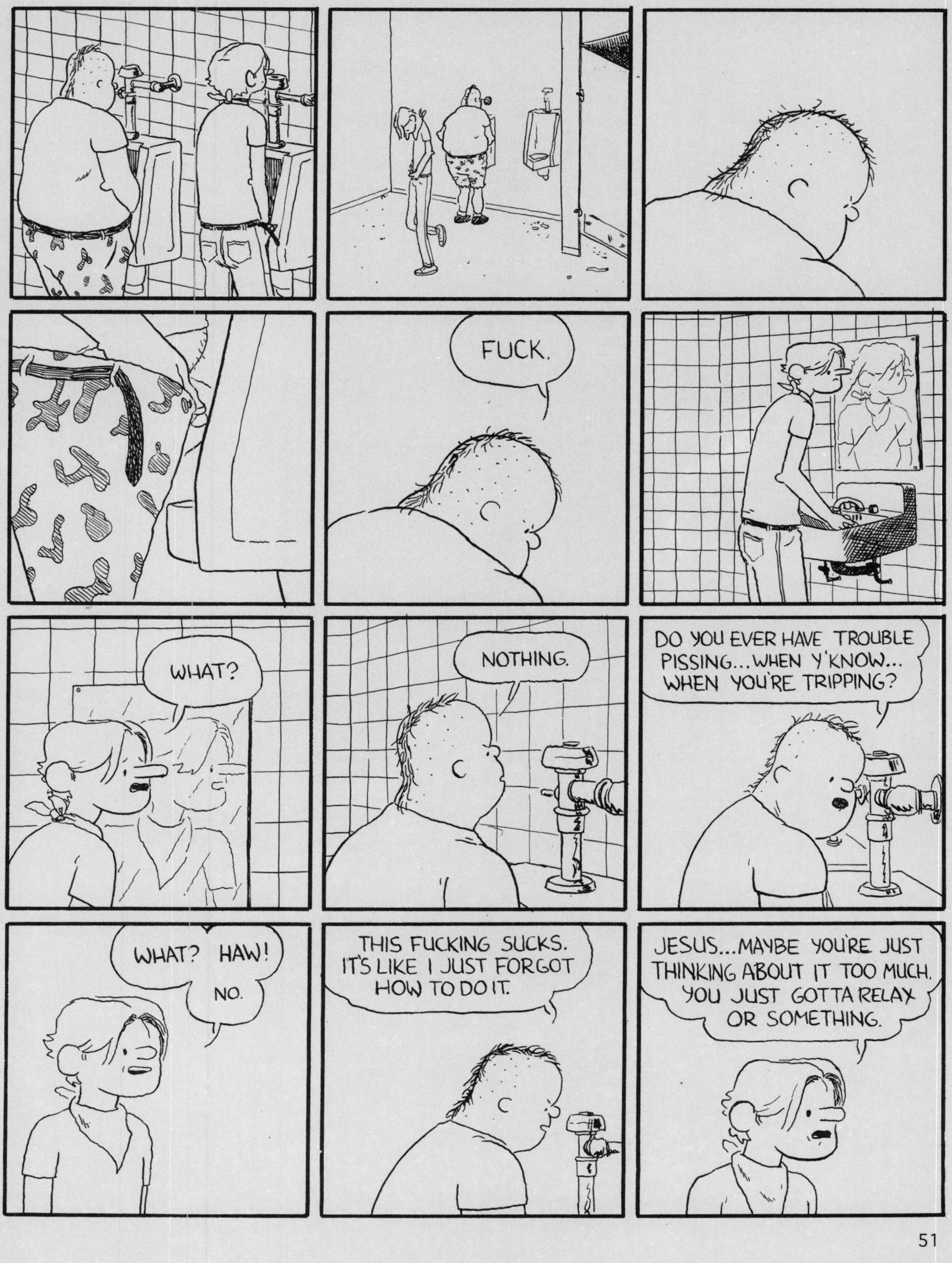
FUCK.
WHAT?
NOTHING.
DO YOU EVER HAVE TROUBLE PISSING...WHEN Y'KNOW... WHEN YOU'RE TRIPPING?
WHAT? HAW!
NO.
THIS FUCKING SUCKS. IT'S LIKE I JUST FORGOT HOW TO DO IT.
JESUS...MAYBE YOU'RE JUST THINKING ABOUT IT TOO MUCH. YOU JUST GOTTA RELAX OR SOMETHING.

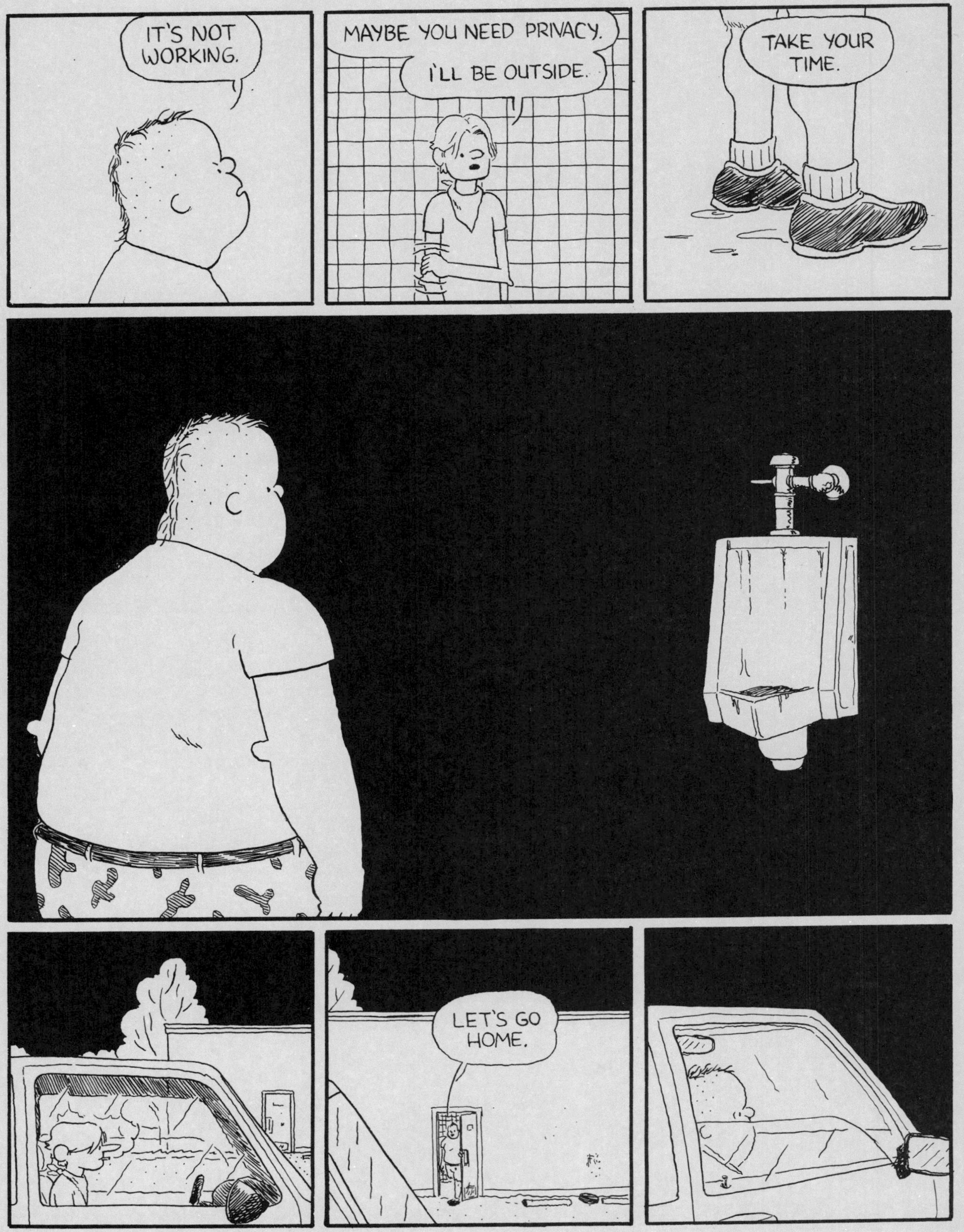
IT'S NOT WORKING.
MAYBE YOU NEED PRIVACY.
I'LL BE OUTSIDE.
TAKE YOUR TIME.
LET'S GO HOME.

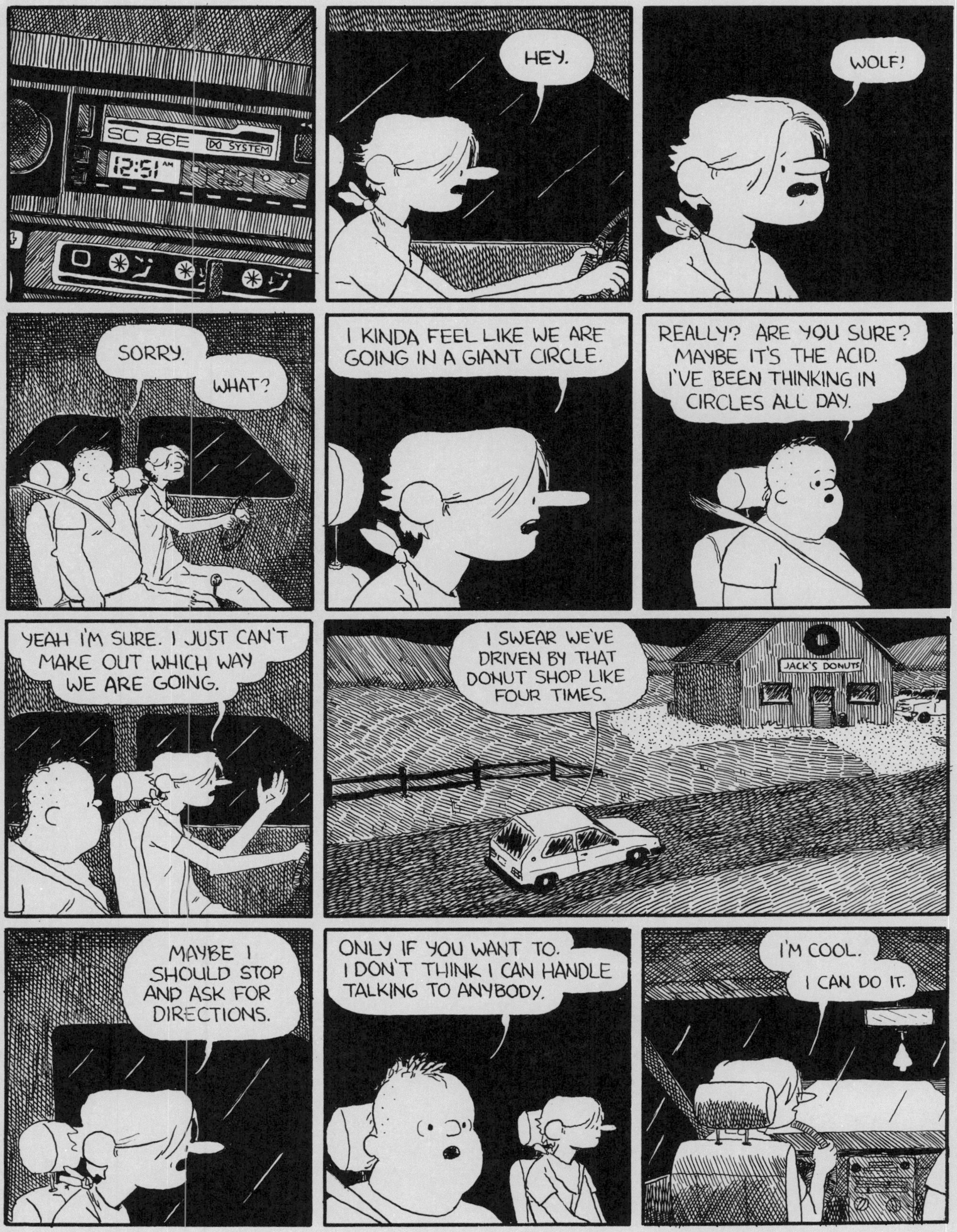
SC 86E
SYSTEM
12:51 AM
HEY.
WOLF!
SORRY.
WHAT?
I KINDA FEEL LIKE WE ARE GOING IN A GIANT CIRCLE.
REALLY? ARE YOU SURE? MAYBE IT'S THE ACID. I'VE BEEN THINKING IN CIRCLES ALL DAY.
YEAH I'M SURE. I JUST CAN'T MAKE OUT WHICH WAY WE ARE GOING.
I SWEAR WE'VE DRIVEN BY THAT DONUT SHOP LIKE FOUR TIMES.
JACK'S DONUTS
MAYBE I SHOULD STOP AND ASK FOR DIRECTIONS.
ONLY IF YOU WANT TO. I DON'T THINK I CAN HANDLE TALKING TO ANYBODY.
I'M COOL.
I CAN DO IT.

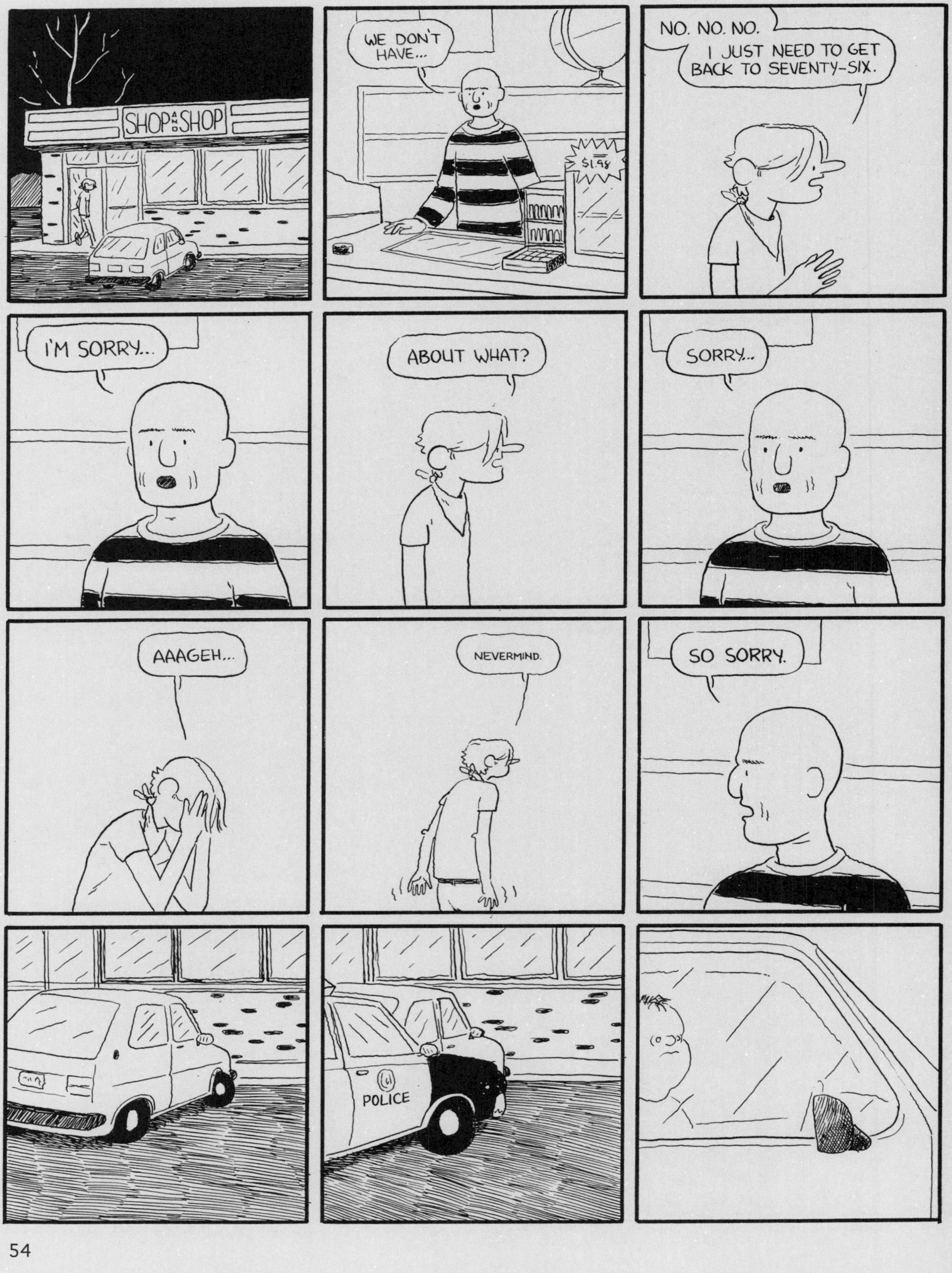
SHOP AND SHOP
WE DON'T HAVE...
$1.98
NO. NO. NO.
I JUST NEED TO GET BACK TO SEVENTY-SIX.
I'M SORRY...
ABOUT WHAT?
SORRY...
AAAGEH...
NEVERMIND.
SO SORRY.
POLICE

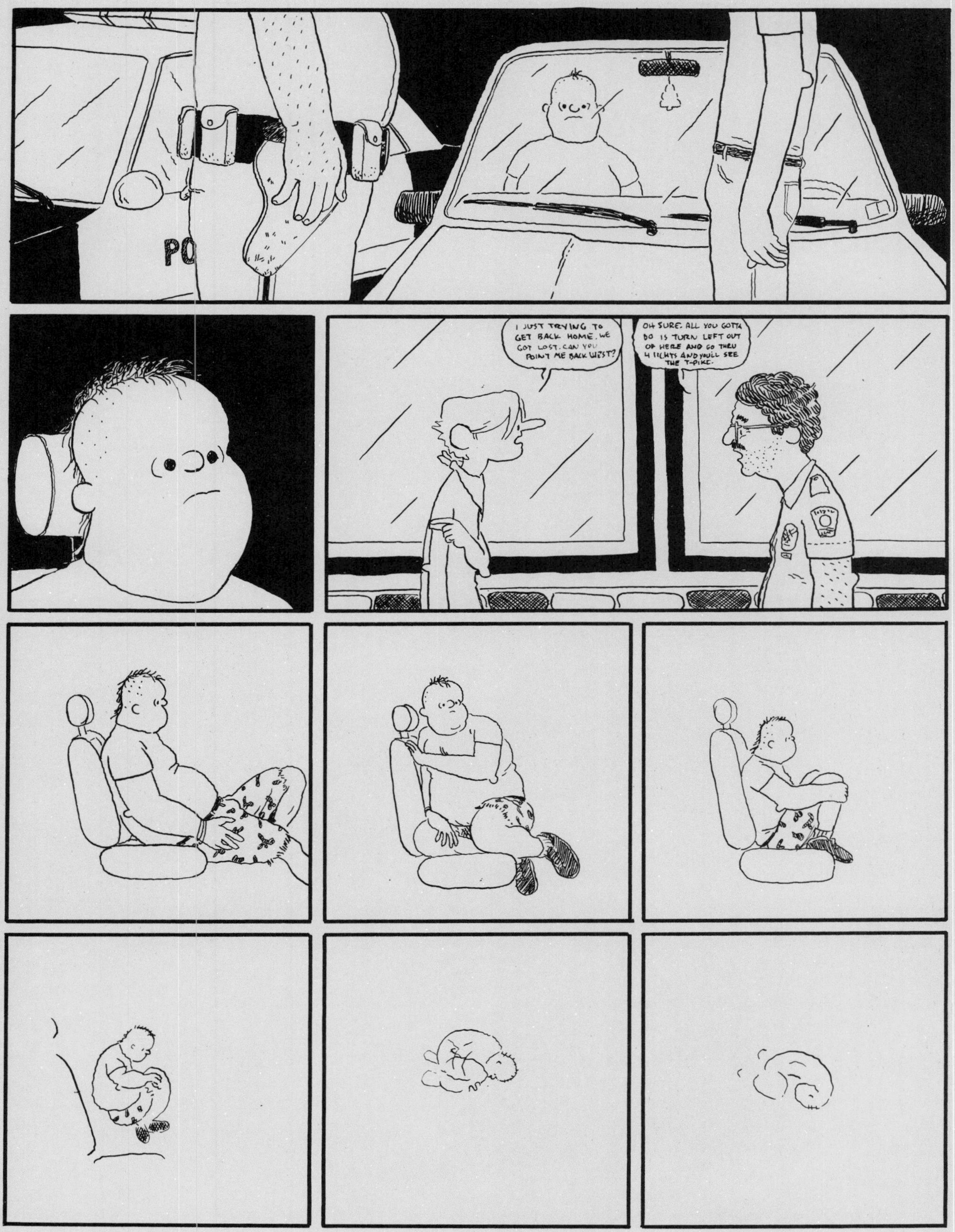
PO
I JUST TRYING TO GET BACK HOME. WE GOT LOST. CAN YOU POINT ME BACK WEST?
OH SURE. ALL YOU GOTTA DO IS TURN LEFT OUT OF HERE AND GO THRU 4 LIGHTS AND YOU'LL SEE THE T-PIKE.

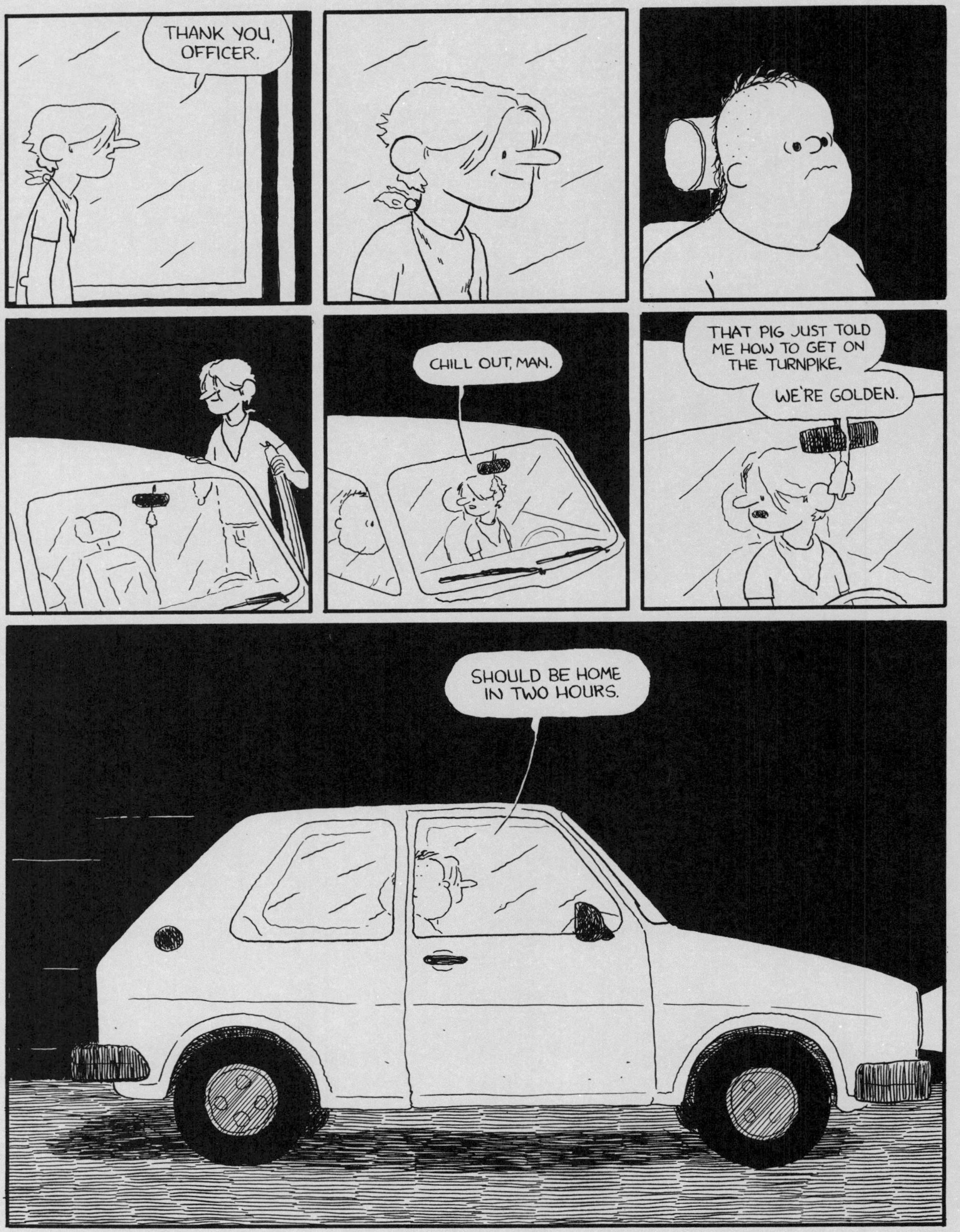
THANK YOU, OFFICER.
CHILL OUT, MAN.
THAT PIG JUST TOLD ME HOW TO GET ON THE TURNPIKE.
WE'RE GOLDEN.
SHOULD BE HOME IN TWO HOURS.

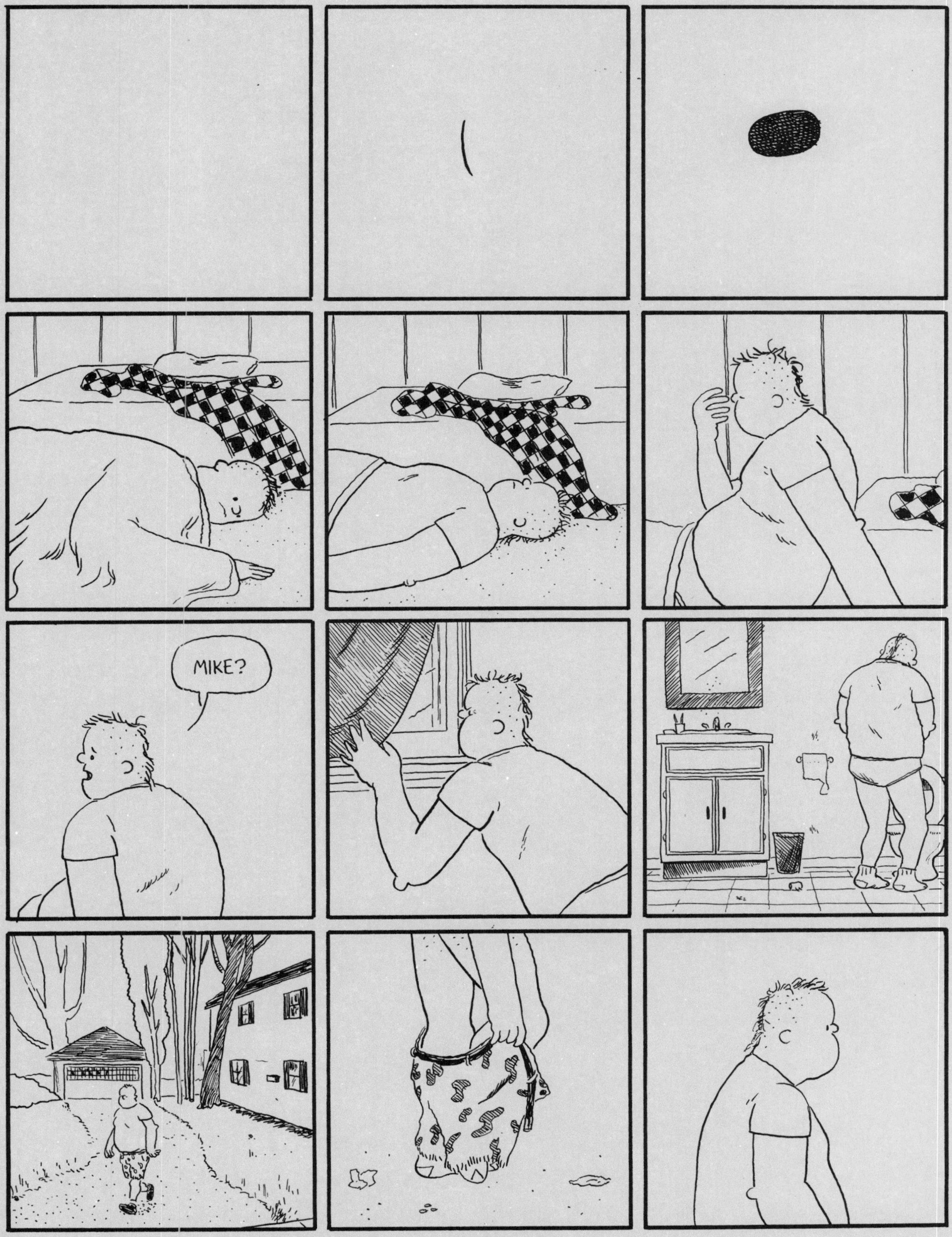
MIKE?

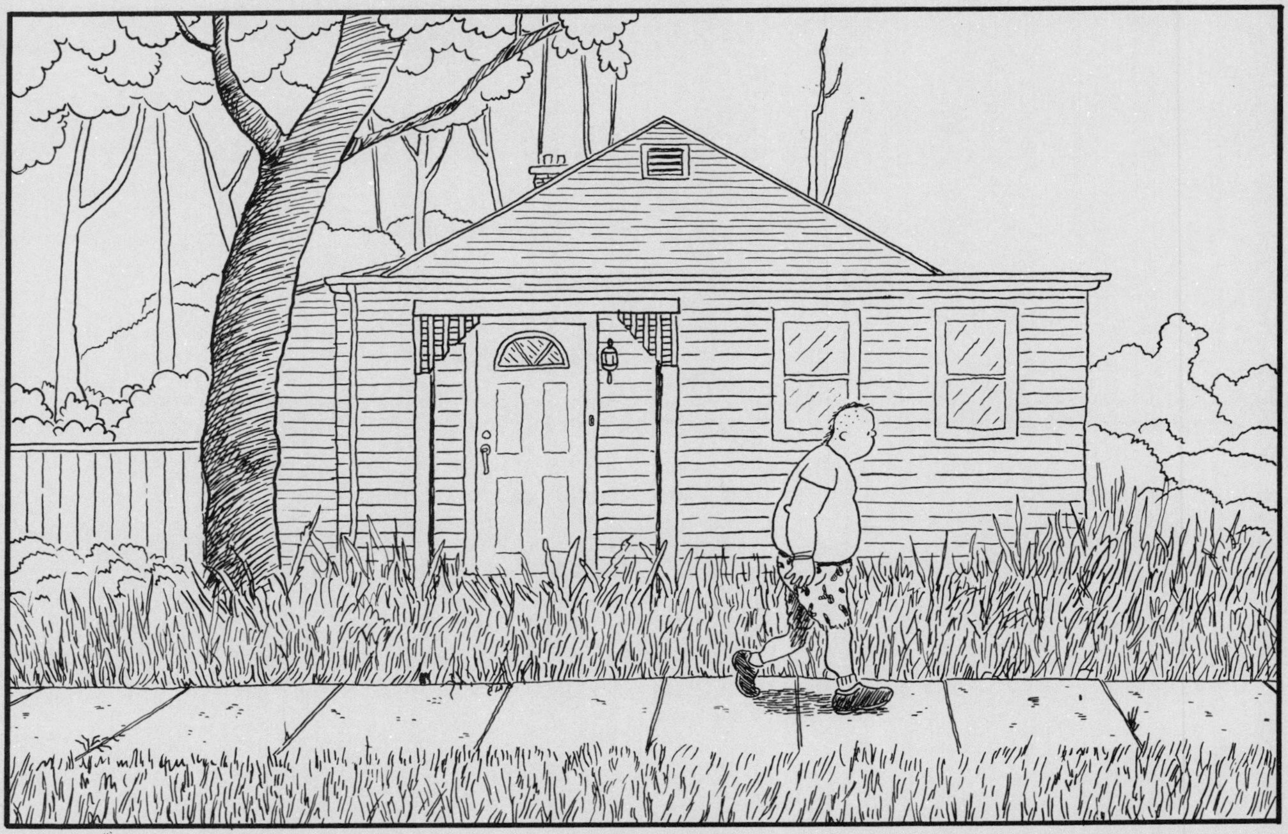

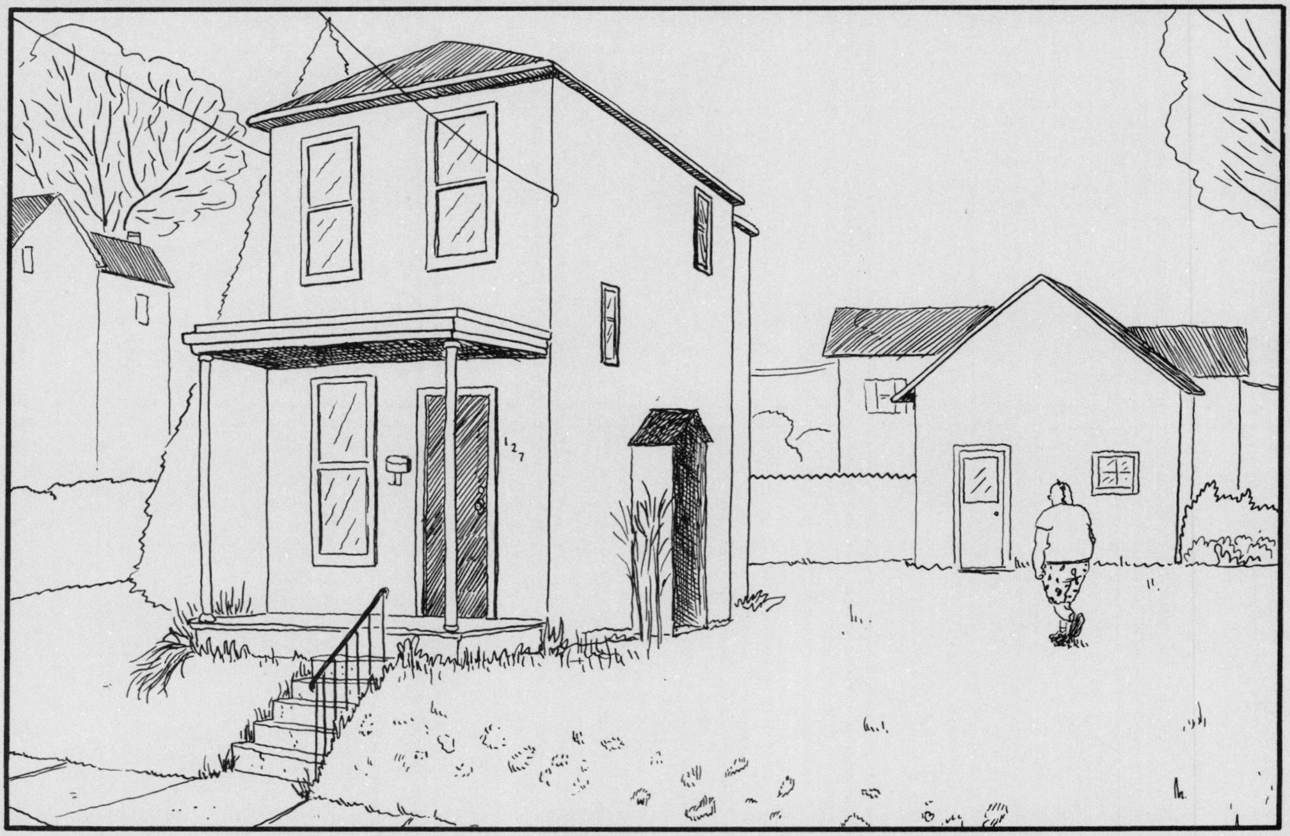
127

 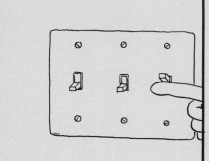 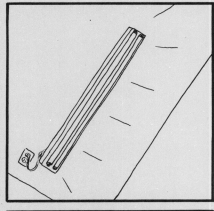

WHEN I WAS 16, GRAMMA LET ME SORT OF TAKE OVER THE GARAGE.

SHE NEVER USED IT MUCH ANYWAYS...

ESPECIALLY AFTER GRAMPA JOHN WENT INTO THE HOSPITAL.

HE USED IT FOR HIS WORKSHOP. LOTS OF TOOLS AND WOOD AND THINGS.

HE MADE ALL THIS WEIRD-LOOKING FURNITURE.

I NEVER SHOWED MUCH INTEREST IN THE STUFF.

SOMETIMES I WISH I HAD.

I JUST USED THE GARAGE TO SLEEP AND PLAY MY TAPES REALLY LOUD.

AND TO HIDE.

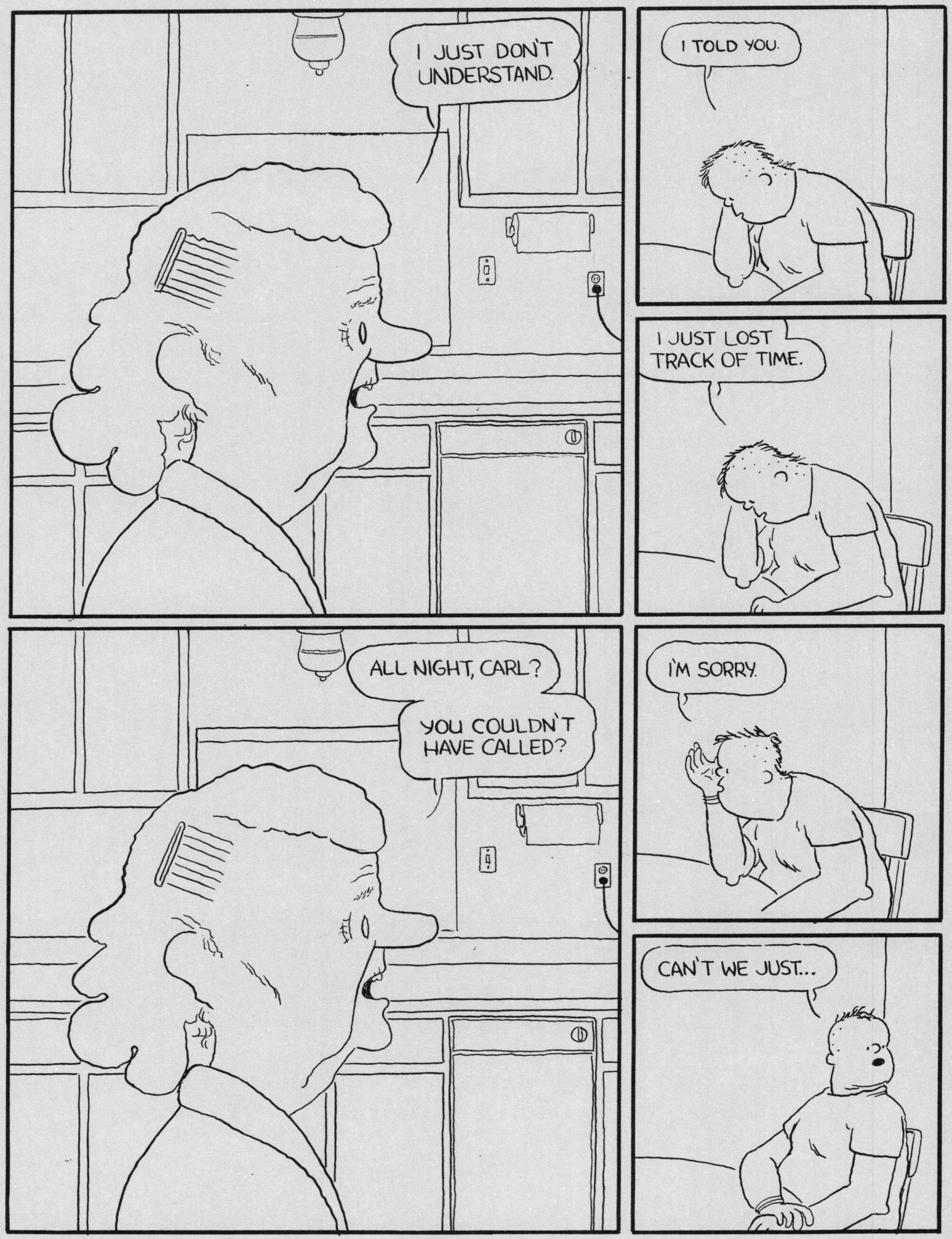
I JUST DON'T UNDERSTAND.
I TOLD YOU.
I JUST LOST TRACK OF TIME.
ALL NIGHT, CARL?
YOU COULDN'T HAVE CALLED?
I'M SORRY.
CAN'T WE JUST...

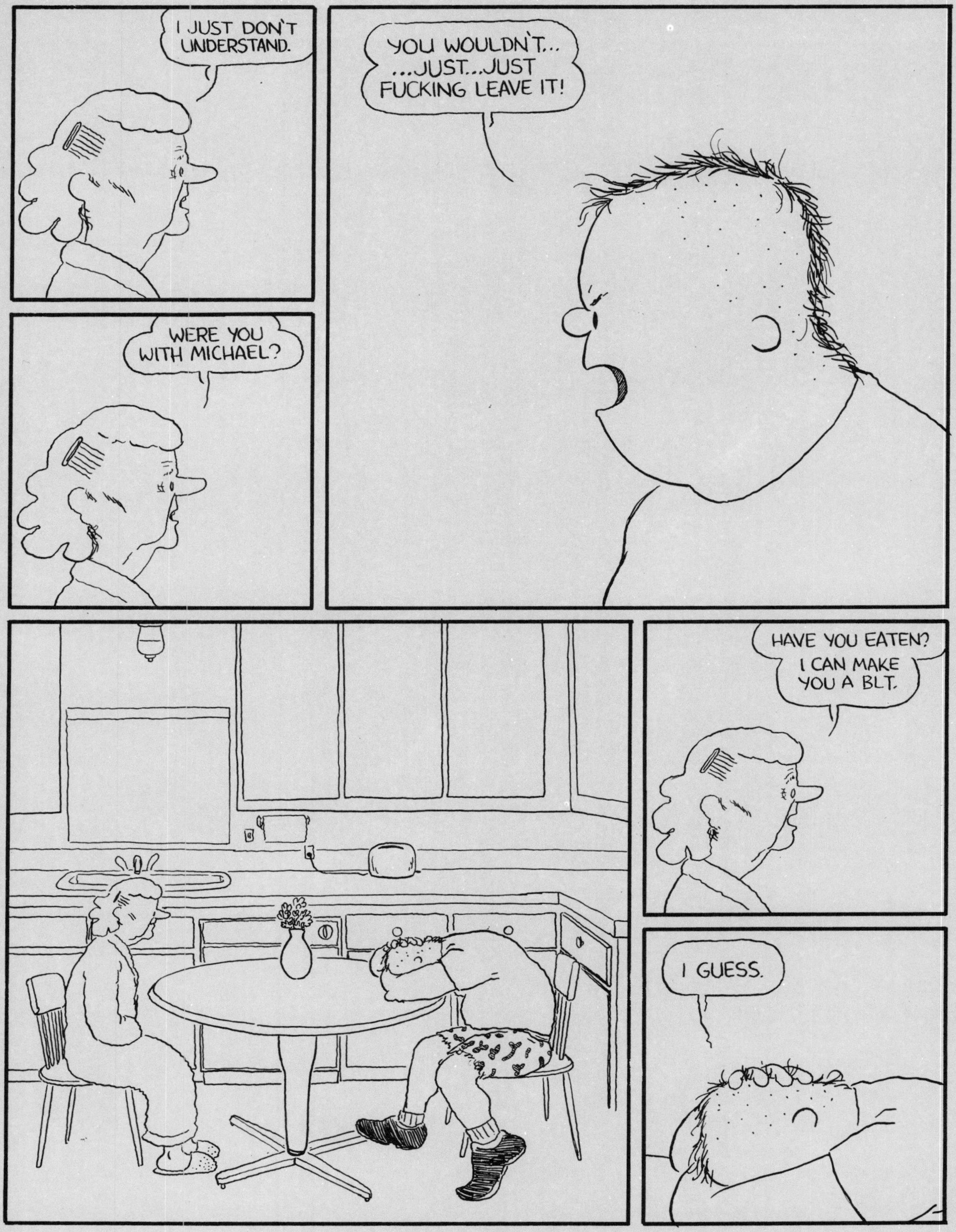
I JUST DON'T UNDERSTAND.
YOU WOULDN'T... ...JUST...JUST FUCKING LEAVE IT!
WERE YOU WITH MICHAEL?
HAVE YOU EATEN? I CAN MAKE YOU A BLT.
I GUESS.

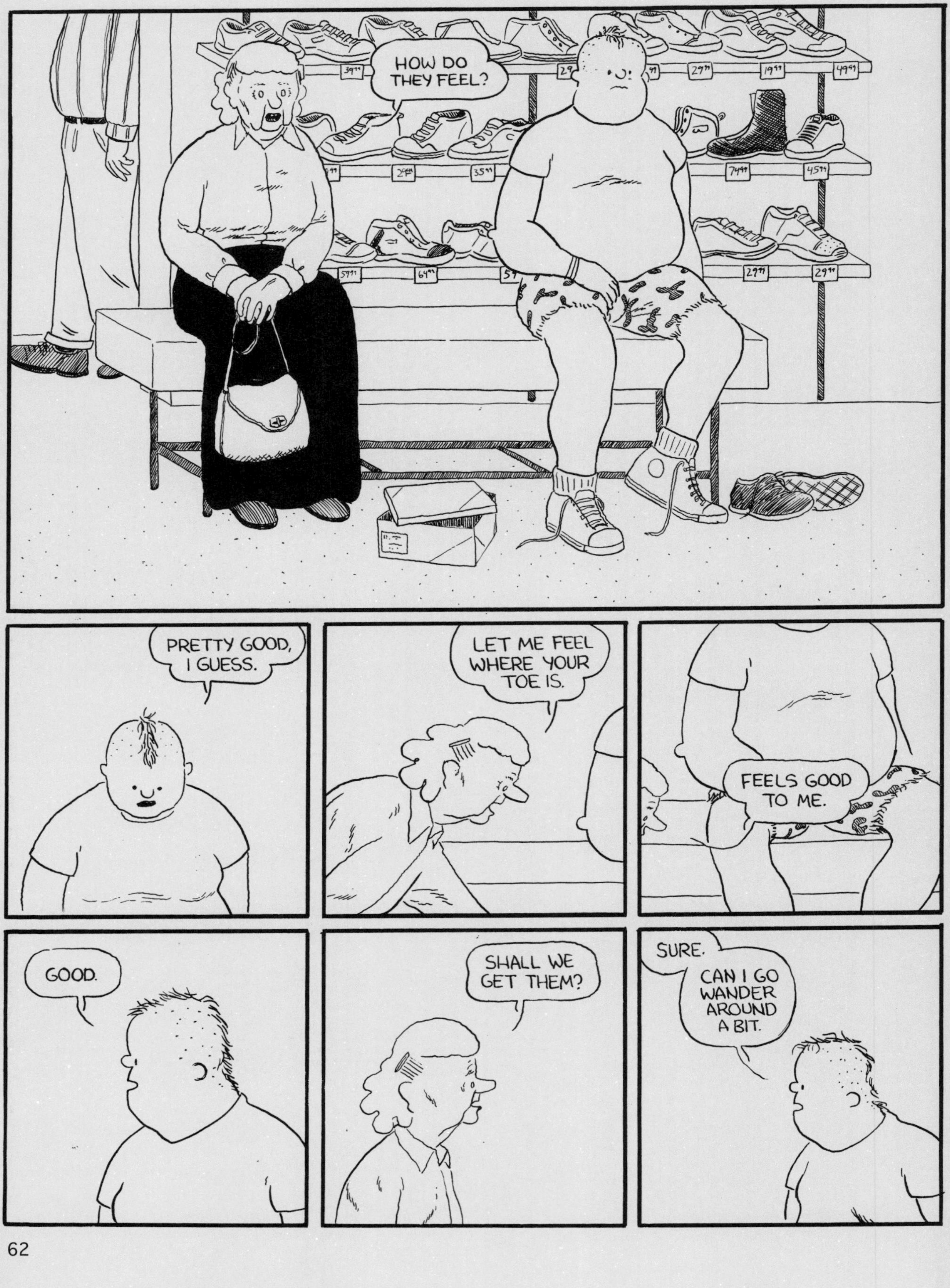
HOW DO THEY FEEL?
PRETTY GOOD, I GUESS.
LET ME FEEL WHERE YOUR TOE IS.
FEELS GOOD TO ME.
GOOD.
SHALL WE GET THEM?
SURE.
CAN I GO WANDER AROUND A BIT.

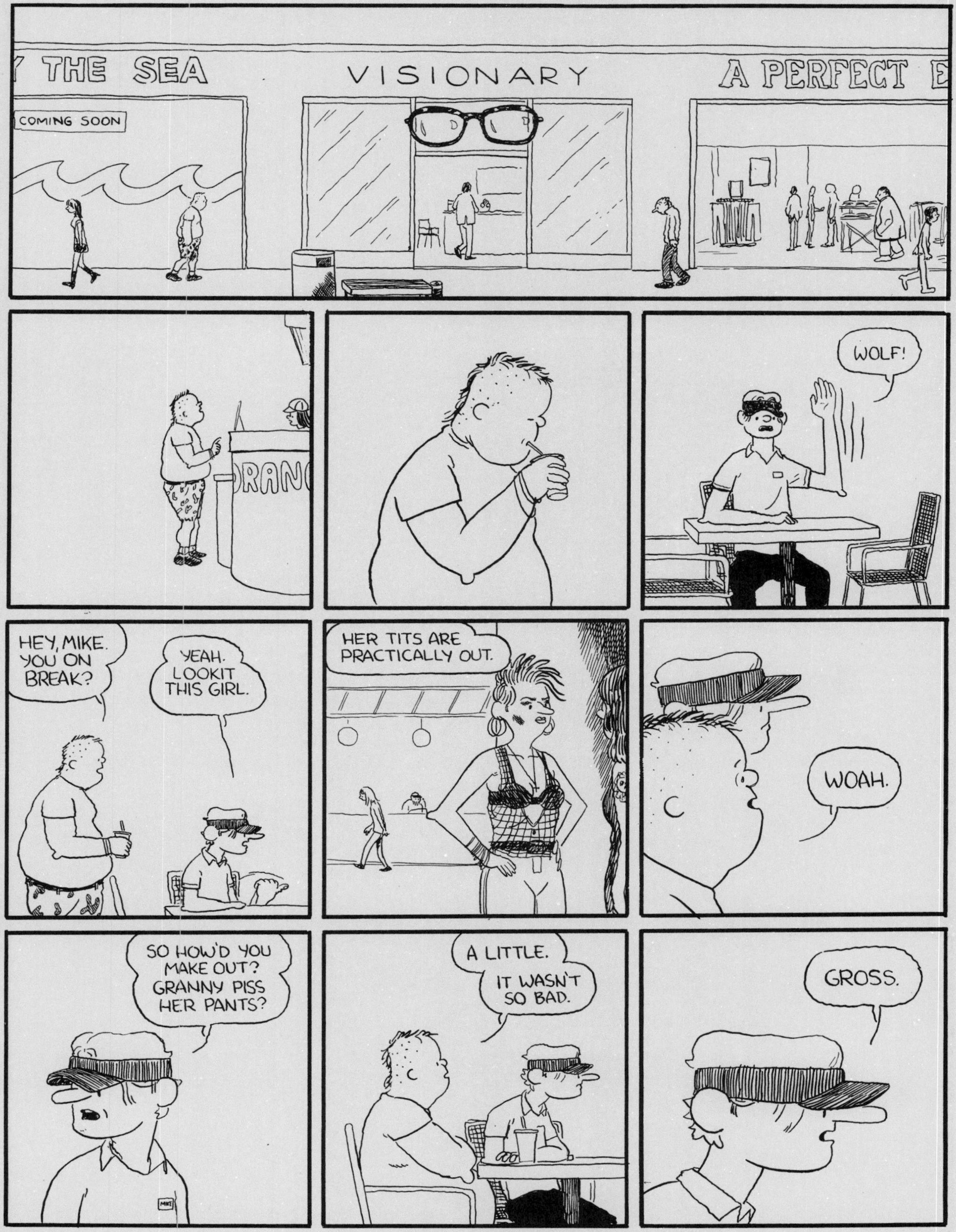

Y THE SEA
VISIONARY
A PERFECT E
COMING SOON
RANG
WOLF!
HEY, MIKE. YOU ON BREAK?
YEAH. LOOKIT THIS GIRL.
HER TITS ARE PRACTICALLY OUT.
WOAH.
SO HOW'D YOU MAKE OUT? GRANNY PISS HER PANTS?
MIKE
A LITTLE.
IT WASN'T SO BAD.
GROSS.

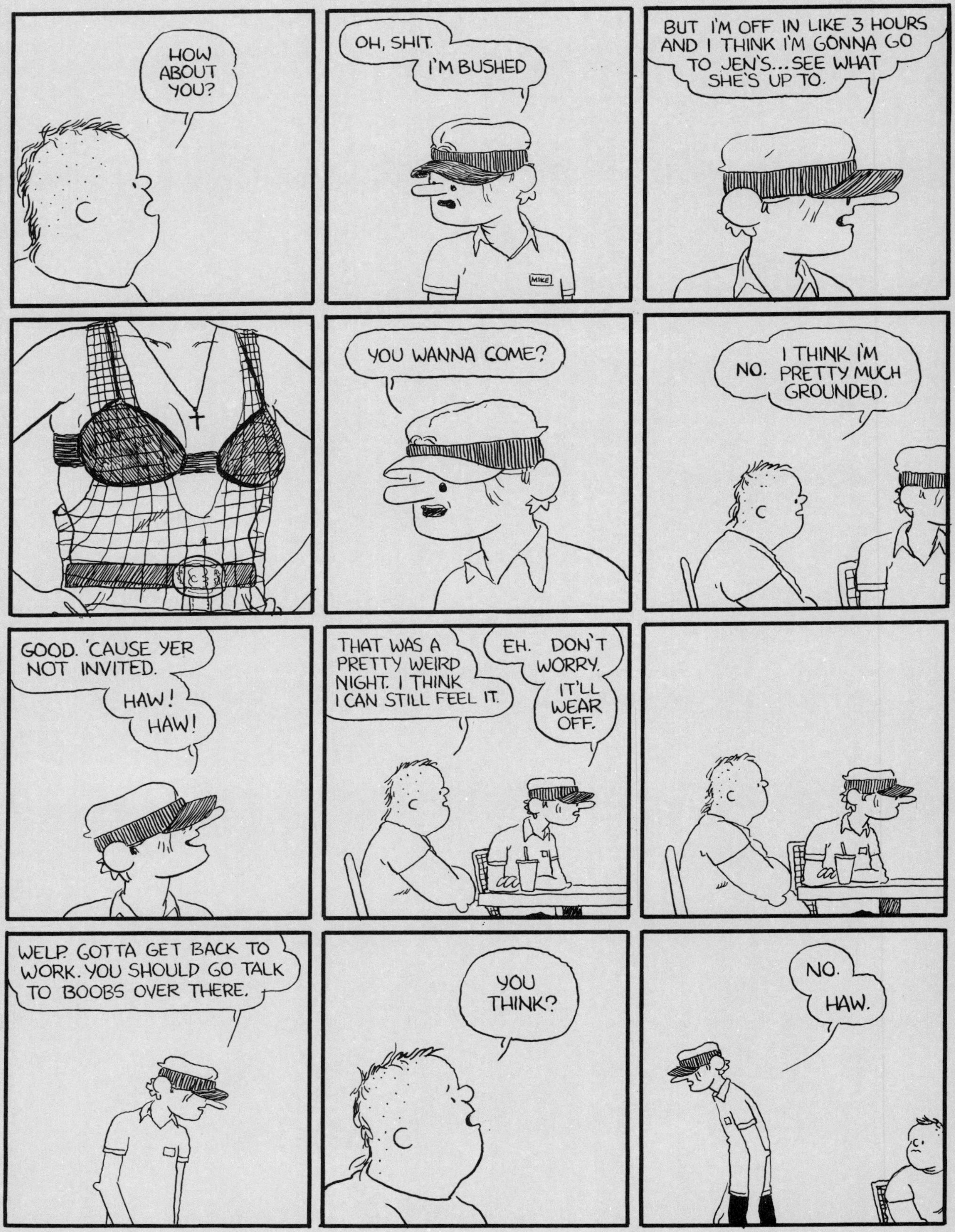
HOW ABOUT YOU?
OH, SHIT.
I'M BUSHED
MIKE
BUT I'M OFF IN LIKE 3 HOURS AND I THINK I'M GONNA GO TO JEN'S...SEE WHAT SHE'S UP TO.
YOU WANNA COME?
NO.
I THINK I'M PRETTY MUCH GROUNDED.
GOOD. 'CAUSE YER NOT INVITED.
HAW! HAW!
THAT WAS A PRETTY WEIRD NIGHT. I THINK I CAN STILL FEEL IT.
EH. DON'T WORRY.
IT'LL WEAR OFF.
WELP. GOTTA GET BACK TO WORK. YOU SHOULD GO TALK TO BOOBS OVER THERE.
YOU THINK?
NO.
HAW.

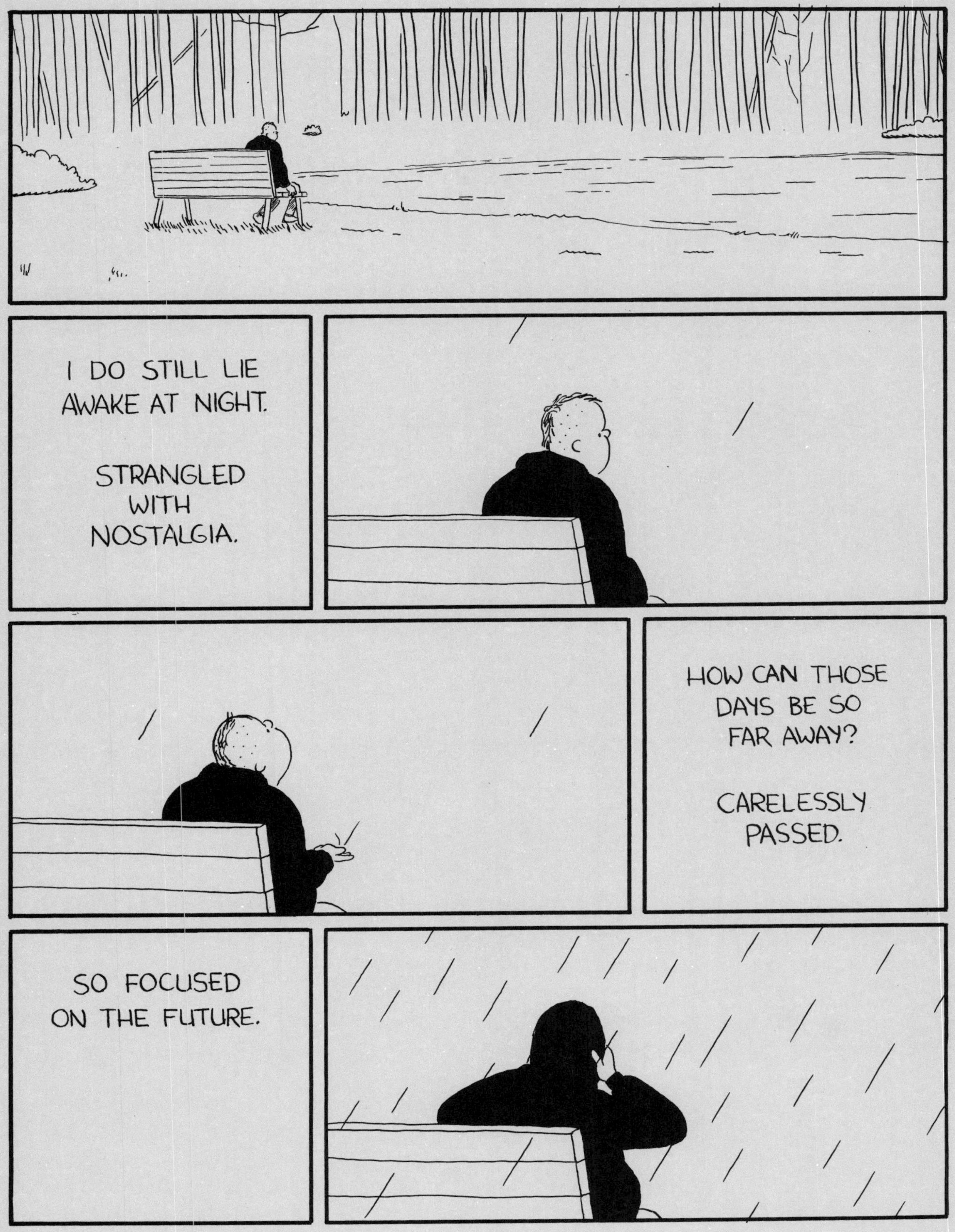
I DO STILL LIE AWAKE AT NIGHT.
STRANGLED WITH NOSTALGIA.
HOW CAN THOSE DAYS BE SO FAR AWAY?
CARELESSLY PASSED.
SO FOCUSED ON THE FUTURE.

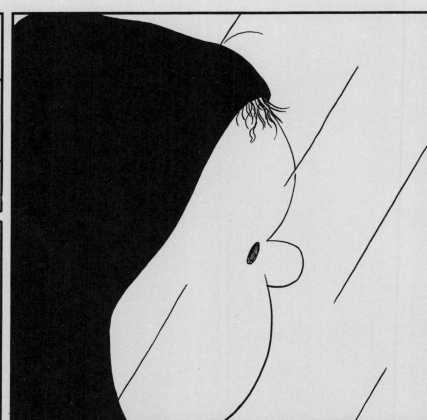

I CAN NEVER
BE THERE AGAIN.

I CANNOT BE
SAVED.

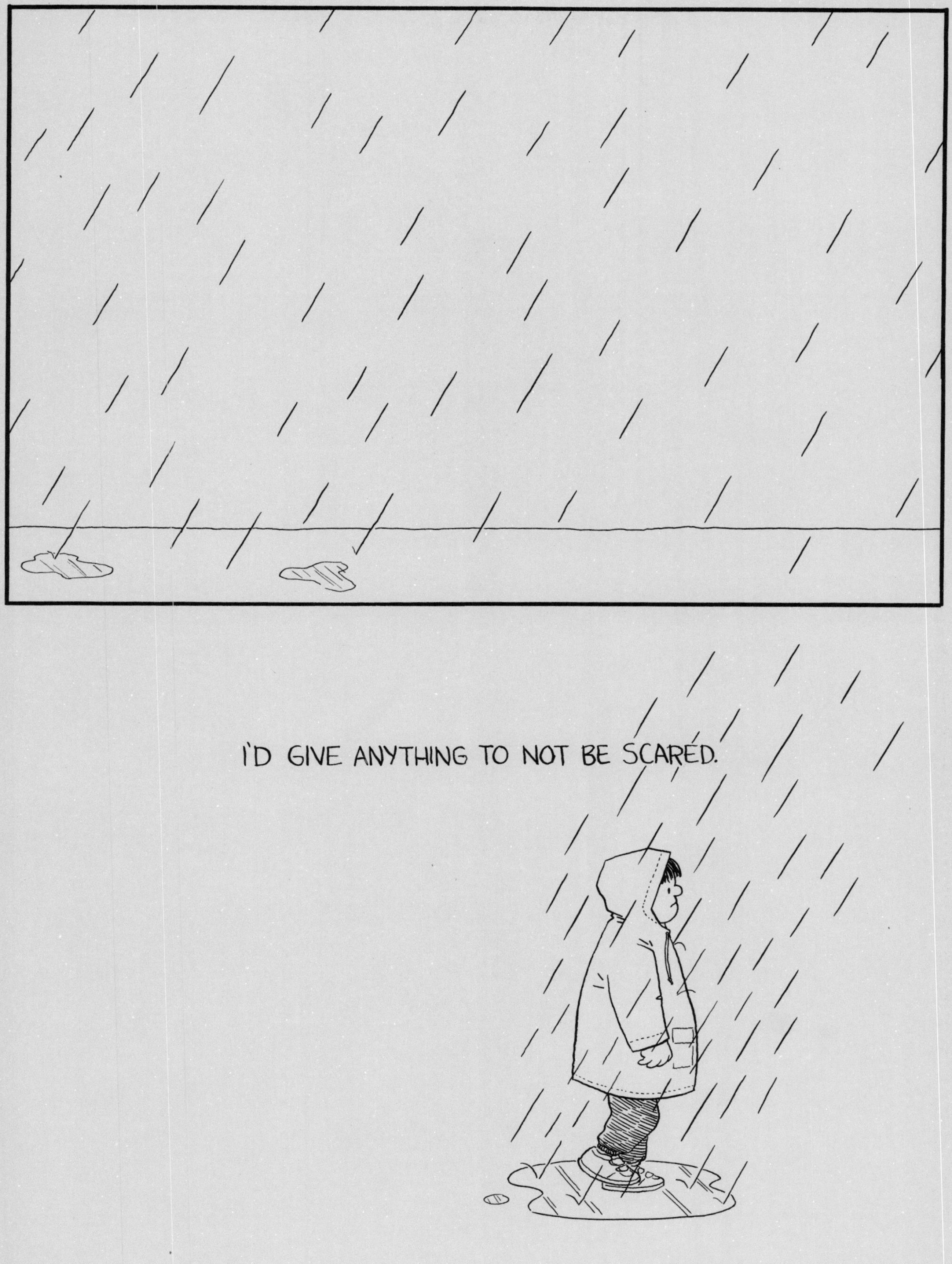
I'D GIVE ANYTHING TO NOT BE SCARED.

CHARLES FORSMAN GREW UP IN MECHANICSBURG, PENNSYLVANIA.

THE AUTHOR WOULD LIKE TO THANK THE FOLLOWING PEOPLE FOR THEIR LOVE, SUPPORT AND INSPRIRATION:

ALYCE FORSMAN, CHARLES FORSMAN (DAD), ZAK FORSMAN, TOBEY FORSMAN, MELISSA MENDES, RYAN GRIFFIN, JUSTIN BARR, RYAN SPAHR, TODD PARADINE, SAMMY HARKHAM, CHESTER BROWN, JAMES STURM, AND MAX DE RADIGUÉS.

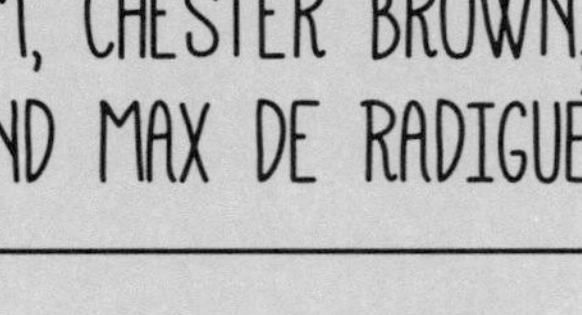

DRAWN IN PROVIDENCE, RHODE ISLAND AND HANCOCK, MASSACHUSETTS BETWEEN MARCH, 2010 AND JANUARY, 2011.

EDITOR & ASSOCIATE PUBLISHER: ERIC REYNOLDS
BOOK DESIGN: CHARLES FORSMAN
PRODUCTION: CHARLES FORSMAN & PAUL BARESH
PUBLISHERS: GARY GROTH & KIM THOMPSON

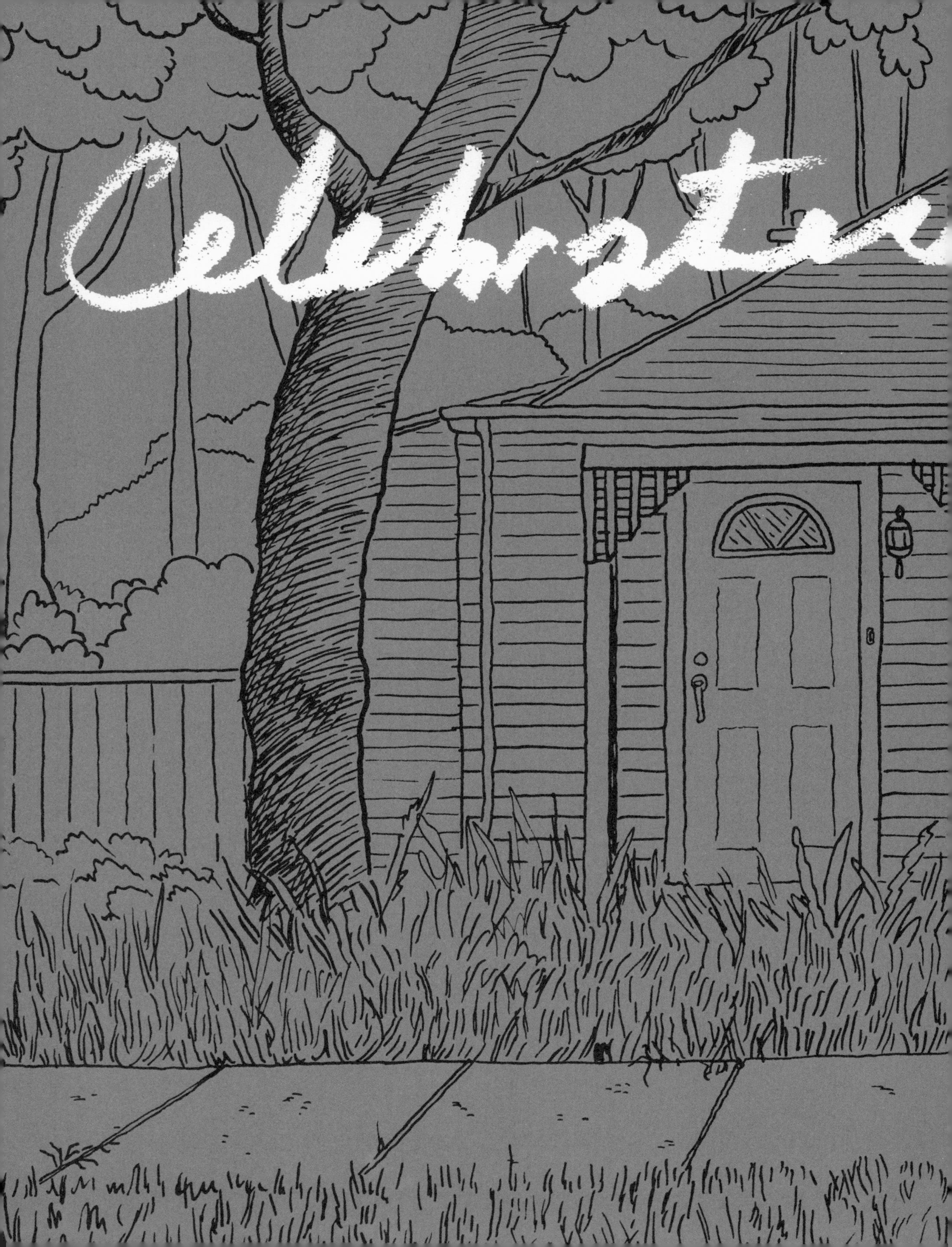
Celebrate